Dieter Götz
Peter O. Lawson

Wirtschaftsenglisch im Kontext von A–Z

Max Hueber Verlag

Das Werk und seine Teile sind urheberrechtlich geschützt.
Jede Verwertung in anderen als den gesetzlich zugelassenen
Fällen bedarf deshalb der vorherigen schriftlichen
Einwilligung des Verlages.

| R 3. 2. 1. | Die letzten Ziffern |
| 2002 2001 2000 1999 | bezeichnen Zahl und Jahr des Druckes. |

Alle Drucke dieser Auflage können, da unverändert,
nebeneinander benutzt werden.
1. Auflage
© 1999 Max Hueber Verlag, D-85737 Ismaning
Verlagsredaktion: Katja Hartmann, München
Satz: Gabriele Stelbrink, Kinsau
Druck und Bindung: Ludwig Auer, Donauwörth
Printed in Germany
ISBN 3-19-002648-3

INHALTSVERZEICHNIS

ABKÜRZUNGEN	8
ABOUT	9
ABOVE – OVER	10
ARBEITSPLÄTZE, ARBEITSLOSIGKEIT	11
ARGUMENTIEREN	18
AT	24
BEDINGUNG, NOTWENDIGKEIT	26
BELOW – UNDER	34
BÖRSE	36
BUSINESS	39
BUT	40
BUY – PURCHASE – SELL – SALE	41
BY	43
CAN – COULD – BE ABLE TO	43
CAPITAL	45
ECONOMIC, ECONOMICS, ECONOMIST, ECONOMY	47
ERWARTEN, SCHÄTZEN, VORAUSSAGEN	50
FINANCE – FINANCIAL	60
GEFAHREN, PROBLEME, SCHWIERIGKEITEN	62
GEGENSATZ, EINRÄUMUNG	69
GEWINNE, EINKÜNFTE	76
INFLATION	82
INTEREST	83
KOSTEN, INVESTITIONEN, SCHULDEN	84
LITTLE – SMALL	92
LOSE – LOSS	94
-LY – ADVERBIEN	95

MANY – MUCH 96
MAY – MIGHT 98
MONEY – MONETARY 101

PLANEN, BEABSICHTIGEN 102

RELATIVSÄTZE 111

'S 113
SHOULD – OUGHT TO 115
STEIGEN, MEHR WERDEN; FALLEN, WENIGER WERDEN; GLEICHBLEIBEN 116
   1. Mehr werden 118
   2. Gleich bleiben 123
   3. Weniger werden 124
   4. Schneller 128
   5. Langsamer 128
STEUER 129
SUBSTANTIVE 132

TERMINOLOGIE 133

UMWELT 135
URSACHEN, FOLGEN, BEGRÜNDUNGEN 137

VALUE – WORTH 146
VERGLEICH, ÄHNLICHKEIT, UNTERSCHIED 147

WERTPAPIERE 159
WILL – WOULD 163
WISSENSCHAFT UND FORSCHUNG 166

ZAHLEN 175
ZEIT 177
   1. Zeitspannen und Zeitpunkte 178
   2. Zeitkonzepte 182
      2.1 Gegenwart 182
      2.2 Vergangenheit 183
      2.3 Zukunft 185
      2.4 Gleichzeitigkeit 185

2.5 Häufigkeit 187
2.6 Dauer 187
3. Präpositionen und Konjunktionen 188
4. Verbformen 191

INDEX BEHANDELTER WÖRTER 193

VORWORT

Wenn im Englischen von Fachsprache oder Fachsprachen die Rede ist, wird der Ausdruck *English for Specific Purposes* verwendet, also ein „Englisch für besondere Zwecke". Mit Bezeichnungen wie *English for Legal Purposes, English for Academic Purposes* oder *English for Economic Purposes* wird dann weiter spezifiziert. Ein so bestimmtes Englisch beinhaltet natürlich eine größere Menge an Fachbegriffen (wie etwa in Wirtschaftstexten *value-added tax* ‚Mehrwertsteuer', *capital flight* ‚Kapitalflucht').

Eine solche Sprache muss aber auch bestimmte Aufgaben erfüllen: „Wirtschaftssprache" muss z.b. darstellen können, wie sich die Wirtschaft entwickeln wird, warum bestimmte Zustände eingetreten sind, wie sich das Auf und Ab über verschiedene Zeiträume verteilt, wie Planungen verlaufen, welche Risiken es gibt, mit welchen Bedingungen man rechnen muss, wie gewisse Konstellationen zu beurteilen sind.

In diesem Nachschlagewerk werden im Wesentlichen die sprachlichen Mittel vorgestellt, die notwendig sind, wenn man sich – in der Fremdsprache Englisch – mit wirtschaftlichen Vorgängen auseinandersetzen will. Dem Buch liegt eine Sammlung von Texten zu Grunde (insgesamt ca. 400.000 Wörter), die der Zeitschrift *The Economist*, Bankberichten und kleineren Quellen entnommen wurden. Die ausgewählten Texte wurden daraufhin untersucht, wie ein bestimmter Bereich (etwa „Gewinne, Einkünfte" oder „Erwarten, Schätzen, Voraussagen" oder „Ursachen, Folgen, Begründungen") sprachlich verwirklicht wird. Sämtliche Beispiele sind authentisch. Die Echtheit der Beispiele bedingt natürlich, dass sie gelegentlich etwas speziell wirken, besonders dann, wenn Namen verwendet wurden. Die Beispiele wurden in der Regel so (teil)übersetzt, dass sie der jeweils vorliegenden Situation entsprechen. Die Übersetzungen sind daher oft relativ „frei", aber gerade darum getreu. In den Fällen, in denen prinzipiell mehrere Übersetzungen möglich waren, wurde diejenige gewählt, die der ursprünglichen Situation des Satzes angemessen erscheint.

Darüber hinaus gibt die Art und Weise der Darstellung des authentischen Sprachmaterials eine Hilfe, wie man Texte selbst sinnvoll liest und mit ihnen arbeitet, um die Techniken zu entwickeln, die für das Lernen einer Fachsprache nötig sind. Um Englisch besser beherrschen zu können, ist es für „fast jede(n)" unabdingbar zu lernen, wie sich das Material angemessen verarbeiten lässt und wie die eigenen Sprachkenntnisse um korrekte Einheiten erweitert werden können. Die Erläuterungen sind so angelegt, dass man lernt, worauf zu achten ist und das Lernenswerte erkennt. Daher ist die Art der Darstellung exemplarisch; nicht alle sach- bzw. sprachspezifischen Bereiche aus Wirtschaft und Finanzwesen konnten berücksichtigt werden.

Es ist auch nicht so, dass von einer einheitlichen Wirtschaftssprache die Rede sein könnte: Wie im Deutschen unterscheiden sich auch im Englischen in sprachlicher Hinsicht Geschäftsbriefe von Börsenberichten, offizielle Bankberichte von Lehrbuchtexten, Wirtschaftskommentare von Steuergesetzen usw. Aus diesem Grund ist es besonders wichtig zu lernen, wie man verschiedene Textsorten „beobachtet", um das jeweils Spezielle zu registrieren und um das eigene Wissen (oder Gespür) hinsichtlich der einzusetzenden sprachlichen Mittel zu vergrößern.

Herrn Peter Lawson, B.Ec., M.A. (Sprachenzentrum der Universität Augsburg) danke ich für seine Unterstützung in fachlichen und sprachlichen Fragen und für die gewissenhafte Durchsicht des Manuskripts. Von ihm stammt auch der Abschnitt „Wertpapiere".

Für Grundbegriffe der Grammatik und des Sprachgebrauchs kann zu Rate gezogen werden: *Englische Grammatik von A - Z* (Max Hueber Verlag 1997) und *Englischer Sprachgebrauch von A - Z* (Max Hueber Verlag 1996).

Dieter Götz

ABKÜRZUNGEN

Abkürzungen sind kein wesentlicher Teil der Wirtschaftsfachsprache, einige werden jedoch verwendet. Von der Aussprache her kann man zwei Typen unterscheiden.

1. Bei den folgenden Abkürzungen werden die Buchstaben einzeln gesprochen, die Betonung liegt auf dem letzten Buchstaben.

EMU Economic and Monetary Union
EPA Environmental Protection Agency
ERM European exchange rate mechanism
FCC Federal Communications Commission
FDI Foreign direct investment
FTA free trade association
GDP gross domestic product
GNP gross national product
IDB Industrial Development Bureau
ICPO International Competition Policy Office
IEA Institute of Economic Affairs
IFS Institute for Fiscal Studies
IIE Institute for International Economics
IMF International Monetary Fund
LBS London Business School
NAS National Academy of Sciences
NYSE New York Stock Exchange
OECD Organisation for Economic Co-operation and Development
PPP purchasing-power parity
SNA system of national accounts
TRIP trade-related intellectual property
VAT Value-Added Tax
WTO World Trade Organisation
WTF World Trade Fund

Außer bei sehr geläufigen Abkürzungen (wie *US, VAT, GDP*) ist es üblich, in einem Text zunächst die volle Form zu geben, wie etwa *Industrial Development Bureau*, und danach, entweder in Klammern oder in einem der folgenden Sätze, die abgekürzte Form zu verwenden, in diesem Falle *IDB*.

2. Die folgenden Abkürzungen werden so ausgesprochen, als seien sie vollständige Wörter.

EFTA European Free Trade Association
GATT General Agreement on Tariffs and Trade
NAFTA North American Free Trade Agreement
NATO North Atlantic Treaty Organisation

R&D ['ɑːrən'diː] ist *research and development*, ‚Forschung und Entwicklung'.
The Fed ist die *Federal Reserve Bank* in den Vereinigten Staaten.

ABOUT

Vor Zahlen. Vor jeder Art von Zahl oder Mengenangabe bedeutet *about* ‚ungefähr, ca.'.
about 4% of Mexico's population
German productivity is about 15% below America's.
by a factor of about 1,000

be about to do something. Diese Konstruktion bedeutet ‚bald, in Kürze etwas tun'.
European leaders may be about to make three big mistakes.
Is Japan about to repeat its mistake?

What about ...? Mit dieser Frage (ohne eine finite Verbform) wird ausgedrückt: ‚Was ist mit X, was geschieht mit X?' (Nicht: **What's about ...*)
What about Britain?
What about 1993?
What about the second argument?
What about investment?

Als Ergänzung. *about* dient als Ergänzung für eine Reihe von Wörtern (Verben, Substantive und Adjektive), die positive/negative Gefühle und Einschätzungen bezeichnen, z.B. *pleased, happy, confident, expectation; to agonise, alarm, anxious, there is something awkward about x, to care, cautious, complain, concern, doubt, fears, to fret, gloom, guess, nervous, to panic, puzzled, to feel queasy.*

consumers' concerns about excessive profits
Economists were fretting about the weakness of the economy.
... puzzled about why real rates have been high.
fears about the impoverishment of unskilled workers

Mit *about* ergänzt werden auch solche Wörter, die sich auf Argumentation/Streit, Information beziehen, z.B. die Substantive *argument, assumption, debate, discussion, dispute, information, judgment* und die Verben *argue, chatter, know, learn, think, talk, say.*
lots of information about his rival
They will know more about the likely costs.
Most economists know even less about technology than they think they do.
Americans talked boldly about boosting investment.
judgments about the future

ABOVE – OVER

Als Adverb. Das Adverb *above* steht unmittelbar nach einem Substantiv, im Sinne von ‚obenstehend, oben genannt'.
see chart above siehe obige Graphik
in the sense defined above wie oben definiert

Das Adverb *over* ist ‚vorüber, vorbei'.
Their problems are all but over ... so gut wie ausgestanden
America's recession is now indisputably over.

Als Präposition (mit Zahl). Sowohl *above* als auch *over* können mit Zahlen verbunden werden, im Sinne von ‚über, mehr als'.
Until inflation gets well above 5%, this cost is not huge.
The true figure is over 12%.

Vor Bruchzahlen steht *over.*
over half of the 500,000 unemployed persons

‚Älter als' geht mit *over* plus Zahl.
the population aged under 15 and over 64

Als Präposition. *above* wird verwendet, wenn es sich um Angaben handelt, die „über" einem bestimmten Niveau oder einer bestimmten Grenze liegen. Substantive nach *above* sind daher z.B. *rates, level, average.*
pay is above average ... über dem Durchschnitt
... if unemployment is above its natural rate ...
Inflation, though tamed, is still above levels in America.
couples with taxable incomes above $140,000
The forecast was above market expectations.

Der häufigste Gebrauch der Präposition *over* ist der im Sinne von ‚während, im Verlauf von, über'.

over the same period
over the next six months
over the past decade
over the year
over the week
over the past two years

over ergänzt Substantive, die ‚Sorge, Argumentation, Diskussion' bezeichnen, also z.B. *controversy, criticism, debate, dispute, discussion, fuss, grievances, uncertainties, worries*. Ferner solche, die ‚Kontrolle, Einfluss' bezeichnen, wie *power, control, influence.*
the discussion over the new FTA
the central banks' influence over economics
fearful of losing control over the yen

ARBEITSPLÄTZE, ARBEITSLOSIGKEIT

employ. *to employ someone* ist ‚jemanden einstellen/ beschäftigen'.
Firms seek to employ more workers.
to employ people on a temporary basis
to protect employed workers

In Verbindung mit *method, analysis*, allgemein mit Vorschriften, bedeutet *employ* ‚gemäß ... handeln, folgen, anwenden'.
a more rigorous analysis employed by economists and social scientists

employee. *an employee* [ɪmˈplɔiː] ist ein Arbeitnehmer (der für ein *salary* oder für *wages* arbeitet).
output per employee
a full-wage employee
employee share ownership Ausgabe von Belegschaftsaktien

employer. *the employer* ist der Arbeitgeber.
the current employer
the present employer
the employer's profit

employment. *employment* wird nicht im Plural gebraucht, ebenso nicht zusammen mit dem unbestimmten Artikel *an*.
Employment has fallen sharply in all Eastern countries. Die Beschäftigung ...
full employment Vollbeschäftigung
overall employment
non-agricultural employment
private sector employment
male employment
employment contract Arbeitsvertrag
employment duration
employment policy
employment rate
employment services Stellenvermittlung
level of employment
people in employment

Der Bereich, für den die Beschäftigung gilt, wird mit der Präposition *in* eingeführt (oder, wie in obigen Beispielen, durch vorangestellte Substantive bzw. Adjektive).
employment in transport and communication
employment in services

Verben, die sich mit *employment* als Substantiv verbinden, sind z.B. *increase, rise, fall*. Solche, die mit *employment* als Objekt gehen, sind z.B. *gain, reduce.*

job. *a job* ist ein Arbeitsplatz, eine Stelle, *jobs* sind die Arbeitsplätze. Sie bilden den *job market* (oder *jobs market*), ‚Arbeitsmarkt'. *jobs* gibt es in bestimmten Bereichen, also *jobs in industry, in services, in banking. People apply for jobs, accept,* *change, find, lose, seek jobs.* Manche Entwicklungen können Arbeisplätze schaffen (*create jobs*), andere können Arbeitsplätze vernichten (*destroy jobs*). Wer einen vollen Arbeitsplatz hat, hat einen *full-time job*, ein Dauerarbeitsplatz ist ein *permanent job*. Arbeitsplätze, die eine hohe Qualifikation verlangen, sind *high-skilled*, andere sind *low(er)-skilled*, letztere sind meist auch *low-paying* oder *low-paid jobs*. Wer kurzzeitarbeitet, ist *on short time (working)* oder *works short time*. Eine Teilzeitbeschäftigung ist *a part-time job* oder *part-time employment*.

jobless. the jobless sind die Arbeitslosen, ihre Zahl wird durch die *jobless rate* ‚Arbeitslosenrate' dargestellt. Die entsprechenden Zahlen *rise, fall, drop* auf einen Wert, *stand at 3%* ‚stehen bei 3%', oder *are 6.8%*. Langzeitarbeitslose sind *long-term jobless*.

labour. Das Substantiv *labour* wird in der Singularform und ohne den unbestimmten Artikel *a* gebraucht.
labour, capital, and raw materials
child labour (die) Kinderarbeit

labour kann ‚schwere Arbeit' bedeuten, also *hard work* (aber *hard labour* ist Zwangsarbeit). In den meisten Fällen ist mit *labour* der Wirtschaftsfaktor Arbeit gemeint.
Bei Verbindungen von *labour* mit einem weiteren Substantiv (wie *labour market*) wird in der Regel das zweite Substantiv betont gesprochen (also *labour MARket*).
cheap labour
unskilled labour
skilled labour
labour costs Lohnkosten
direct labour costs direkte Lohnkosten
labour force Belegschaft, Arbeitskräfte
labour market Arbeitsmarkt
labour productivity Arbeitsproduktivität
labour standards Arbeitsbedingungen
labour supply verfügbare Arbeitskräfte
labour turnover Arbeitsplatzwechsel

self – employment. self-employment ist die selbständige Tätigkeit.
the growth in/of self-employment during the 1980s
some people choose self-employment

Die entsprechende Bevölkerungsgruppe wird als *the self-employed* bezeichnet.
The self-employed are a significant slice of the workforce.
The number of self-employed almost doubled over this period.

underemployment. *underemployment* bezeichnet den Zustand, wenn jemand nicht genügend Arbeit hat, um davon leben zu können, auch eine Wirtschaftslage, in der weniger als Vollbeschäftigung besteht.

unemployed. *unemployed* ‚arbeitslos, ohne Beschäftigung' wird als Adjektiv verwendet.
unemployed workers
If somebody is unemployed ...
Helping the unemployed was easy.

the unemployed sind die Arbeits-/Beschäftigungslosen.
the long-term unemployed
Instead of paying the unemployed to stay at home, why not pay the same money as a subsidy to encourage firms to hire them?

unemployment. *unemployment* wird nicht im Plural gebraucht, ebenso nicht zusammen mit dem unbestimmten Artikel *an*.
A second reason why unemployment is low ... warum die Arbeitslosigkeit ...
actual unemployment tatsächliche Arbeitslosigkeit
aggregate unemployment Gesamtbeschäftigungslosigkeit
duration of unemployment
high unemployment
long-term unemployment
low unemployment
natural unemployment
private-sector unemployment ... in der Privatwirtschaft
rise of unemployment
structural unemployment
unemployment rate, rate of unemployment
unemployment benefits Arbeitslosenunterstützung
youth unemployment Jugendarbeitslosigkeit

Der Bereich, für den die Arbeitslosigkeit gilt, wird mit der Präposition *in* eingeführt.
unemployment in airlines

Die wichtigsten Verben, die *unemployment* als Subjekt haben, sind *fall, rise, increase, decrease, peak*. *Unemployment* mit Objekt geht mit *reduce, keep down, cut*.

work Verb. Wenn man von Personen sagt, *they work,* dann ist gemeint, ‚dass sie in einem Beschäftigungsverhältnis stehen‘.
people who work for someone else
the incentive to work
the unemployed that really want to work

Mit *work* kann aber auch eine Tätigkeit (das tatsächliche Arbeiten) bezeichnet werden.
Why work harder to earn more?
[People who] work a minimum of 50 hours a week.
The self-employed tend to work longer hours.

Die häufigste Verwendung von *work* ist jedoch die, dass man von etwas sagt, *it works (somehow)* ‚es erfüllt (auf irgendeine Weise) seinen Zweck, funktioniert, ist sinnvoll‘, oft in Verbindung mit Adverbien wie *well, efficiently, better*.
How would this work? Wie könnte das gehen, aussehen, funktionieren?
This is how it would work.
Some types of aid may work better than others.
Will it work?
The model appears to work well.

work out something bedeutet ‚etwas herausfinden, ermitteln, untersuchen‘.
The necessity of working out feasible policies. ... eine durchsetzbare Politik zu erarbeiten.

work Substantiv. *work* (nur im Singular, ohne den unbestimmten Artikel *a*) bezeichnet den Zustand der (abhängigen) Beschäftigung.
people out of work
people in work
to find work
to seek work
to take work annehmen

work incentives Arbeitsanreize
work permit Arbeitserlaubnis

Weiterhin ist *work* (nur im Singular) die Arbeit, die jemand tut.

work-habits
work-shy arbeitsscheu
hard work
the hours available for work

Theoretische Arbeit über etwas ist *work (on)*.
... to start work on a treaty on global climate change.

Im Zusammenhang mit Namen (oder den Possessivpronomen *his, her* usw.) ist *work* eine Arbeit im Sinne von Untersuchung, Abhandlung, Buch, Werk – in dieser Bedeutung auch im Plural.
But Mr Nash's work needed refining.
his latest work
His works suggests that ... Seine Arbeiten ...
Keynes's most influential work, his 1936 "General Theory of Employment, Interest and Money"

Von Faktoren, Entwicklungen kann man sagen, *they are at work,* d.h. ‚sie spielen eine Rolle, machen sich bemerkbar'.

worker. *a worker* kann allgemein ‚eine Arbeitskraft, eine(n) Arbeitnehmer(in)' bezeichnen, aber auch ‚Arbeiter(in)'. Das Wort ist – anders als im Deutschen ‚der Arbeiter' – geschlechtsneutral.
Die Verwendung im Singular ist selten.
Nearly half of America's workers are women.
the average worker
existing workers bislang Beschäftigte
factory workers
full-time worker
highly educated, skilled workers
jobless workers
low-skilled, low-paid workers
male workers
non-production (white-collar) workers
production (blue-collar) workers
oppressed workers
steel workers

suitable workers geeignet
trained workers ausgebildet
unemployed workers
university-educated workers
unskilled workers

Workers achieve productivity, demand higher wages, lose their jobs, have to change their jobs, retire, produce, seek jobs, accept a job.
Workers can be hired, employed, fired, sacked. *worker mobility* wird verlangt.

workforce. *the workforce* ist die Belegschaft eines Unternehmens, auch der erwerbstätige Teil der Bevölkerung.
the firm's worldwide workforce
A third of Eastern Germany's workforce is either unemployed or on short-time working.

working. *working* ist das Partizip Präsens zum Verb *work*, aber auch ein Substantiv für sich (nur im Singular, also ohne den unbestimmten Artikel *a*).
Es kann für ‚Bearbeitung, Verarbeitung' stehen.
car, car-parts and metal-working industries

Es steht nach Präpositionen, die keinen Infinitiv nach sich haben.
... which prevented markets from working efficiently
legal barriers to working for a living
(*barriers* mit *to* verlangt nach einem anschließenden Substantiv, daher *working* und nicht *work*.)

Es steht für ‚Arbeit = das Arbeiten'.
short-time working
Working for yourself
the gain from working

Schließlich werden mit *working* – eher als mit *work* – komplexere Ausdrücke gebildet, wie etwa
working age
working class
working hours Arbeitszeit
working mobility
working paper Arbeitspapier/-vorlage

17

ARGUMENTIEREN

Siehe auch PLANEN, BEABSICHTIGEN und URSACHEN, FOLGEN, BEGRÜNDUNGEN

accept. Das Verb *accept* kann im Sinne von ‚zugeben, eingestehen' verwendet werden.
They are reluctant to accept that there will be many losers.

affair. Im Sinne von ‚Sache, Angelegenheit' wird *affair* kaum verwendet (siehe dazu *matter* in diesem Abschnitt). Mit *affairs* kann man sich auf die wichtigen Dinge innerhalb eines genannten Bereiches beziehen.
defence and foreign affairs
Institute of Economic Affairs (IEA)

agree. Siehe *agree* in PLANEN, BEABSICHTIGEN.

argue. to argue ist ‚argumentieren'. Man kann *against something* oder *for something* argumentieren.
He has already argued for a tax on utilities.

they argued oder he argued oder it is argued usw. wird häufig zwischen Kommas eingeschoben. Bei einem einfachen Subjekt kann auch umgestellt werden (drittes Beispiel).
This is true, Ms Tyson argues, in two ways.
So it is essential, they argue, for the rich countries to supply aid to the region.
The irony is, argues Mr McKinnon, that ...

In den meisten Fällen wird *argue* von einem *that*-Satz gefolgt. Im *that*-Satz stehen auch Modalverben wie *will, may, might* usw.
Many argue that foreign aid is a waste of money.
They argue that the deal will actually benefit developing countries.
They argue that rational investors may follow others whom they think are better informed. ... dass rational entscheidende Investoren wahrscheinlich denjenigen folgen, von denen sie glauben, sie seien besser informiert.

argument. Eine öffentliche, auch in der Presse geführte Diskussion kann als *argument* bezeichnet werden.
The argument is really about jobs.
[This] has set off a great argument. Das hat zu einer großen Diskussion geführt.
an argument ist jedoch meistens das, was man sagt, um andere zu überzeugen, ein Argument (*for* ‚für', *against* ‚gegen').
The argument runs as follows.
The argument is that ...
The argument that a moral obligation to future generations demands special treatment of environmental investments is fatuous. ... ist völlig unsinnig.
..., the argument goes, ... so das Argument

case. Siehe *case* in BEDINGUNG, NOTWENDIGKEIT.

convince. *to convince someone* (*of something*) ist ‚jemanden (von etwas) überzeugen'. Es kann auch als *convince someone* mit *that*-Satz konstruiert werden.
It might be still harder to convince congressmen that the central bank knows what it is doing.
Dazu das Adjektiv *convincing* ‚überzeugend': *convincing proof, convincing evidence.* Dazu auch das Adjektiv *convinced.*
Economists are not entirely convinced. ... nicht völlig uberzeugt.

debate. *a debate* ist eine Diskussion, Debatte, die sich in der Öffentlichkeit abspielt.
the G7's debate about the shape of future aid
the debate over labour standards die Debatte über Arbeitsbedingungen
a broader debate on how useful the money supply is for setting economic policy
Adjektive und *debate*: *broad* (allgemein), *endless*, *heated* (hitzig), *lively*.
the environmental debate ist die Umweltdiskussion.
Das Adjektiv *debatable* bedeutet ‚umstritten, unsicher'.
This is debatable, to put it mildly. ... um es zurückhaltend auszudrücken.

deny. *to deny something* ist ‚abstreiten'.
It has never been denied in these pages.
VW denied the charges. ... bestritt die Vorwürfe.

This is not to deny that consumers have had much to worry about. Damit wird nicht abgestritten/bestritten, dass ...

to deny someone something oder *to deny something to someone* ist ‚jemandem etwas verweigern'.

discuss. *to discuss something* ist ‚etwas bereden, verhandeln, diskutieren'. (Es wird nicht mit *over* oder *about* ergänzt.)
Mexico is discussing a free-trade agreement.
Mr Williamson's ideas were much discussed.

Das Substantiv *discussion* wird mit *about* oder *over* ergänzt.
the GATT's discussion about the environment
the discussion over the new FTA

Something is under discussion bedeutet, dass noch über etwas verhandelt wird.

emphasis. *emphasis* ['emfəsɪs] ‚Betonung, Nachdruck' kann mit *on* ergänzt werden. ‚Nachdruck auf etwas legen' ist *put/place emphasis on something*. Das Verb *to emphasise* ['emfəsaɪz] wird mit einem folgenden Substantiv oder mit einem *that*-Satz konstruiert.

important. Das Adjektiv *important* wird häufig zusammen mit *more* oder *most* gebraucht.
one of the most important tasks in economics

more/most important werden auch zu Anfang des Satzes verwendet, ‚was noch wichtiger/am wichtigsten ist'.
More important, the schemes cost money.

Das Substantiv *importance* wird mit *of* ergänzt.
the importance of exchange rates

insist. Das Verb *insist* ‚bestehen auf, großen Nachdruck legen auf' wird mit *on* oder einem *that*-Satz konstruiert.
insisting on Western safety standards
Mr Clinton should insist that the British media adopt quotas.

Das Substantiv ist *insistence* (*on/that* ...).

issue. *an issue* ist ein meist wichtiges Thema, das gerade zur Diskussion steht: *a controversial, intriguing, political, pressing issue.*
[He] sets out the issues with a new clarity.
Your review raised another issue. ... hat ein anderes Problem aufgeworfen ...
an issue of great interest eine Frage von großer Bedeutung
issues in global politics

an issue ist ferner die (tägliche, wöchentliche usw.) Ausgabe einer Zeitschrift. Mit *issue* wird auch das Ausgeben von Aktien, Währungen, Briefmarken usw. bezeichnet (dazu dann das Verb *to issue*).

matter. *the matter* ist das gerade besprochene Thema, das Problem.
Mr Blackhurst thinks the matter is not so clear-cut.

matter wird in einigen Wendungen gebraucht.
a matter of life and death/time/money eine Angelegenheit, bei der es um Leben und Tod geht; eine Frage der Zeit/des Geldes
[This] is another matter. Das ist wieder eine andere Sache.
no matter how gleichgültig wie

Das Verb *to matter* ist ‚wichtig sein, eine Rolle spielen'.
But its imports are what matter. Aber die Importe sind es, die eine Rolle spielen.
Does it matter whether/how/if ... Spielt es eine Rolle, ob/wie/wenn ...

Something matters to someone ist ‚etwas betrifft, tangiert jemanden'.

mention. *to mention something* ist ‚etwas erwähnen', auch mit einem folgenden *that*-Satz konstruiert. Die Wendung *not to mention x* bedeutet ‚ganz zu schweigen von x'.

persuade. *persuade* ist ‚überreden, überzeugen'. Es wird mit Objekt und einem anschließenden *to*-Infinitiv oder einem anschließenden *that*-Satz konstruiert.
If America had not persuaded Japan to limit its exports ...
Russia needs to be persuaded that the success of its own reforms will depend on keeping trade flowing among the republics. Russland muss davon überzeugt werden, dass ...

point Substantiv. Im Zusammenhang mit Argumentieren ist *a point* ‚ein Punkt'.
the crucial point (is that) der entscheidende Punkt (ist, dass)
an important point
the second point
up to a point bis zu einem gewissen Punkt
from this point of view
a basic point
to miss the point an der Sache vorbeigehen
beside the point an der Sache vorbei
to have a point Recht haben (an einem Punkt der Argumentation)
from this point on ab diesem Punkt

point kann auch ‚Zweck' bedeuten.
There is little point in trying ... Es hat wenig Sinn/Zweck, es mit ... zu versuchen.

Das Adjektiv *pointless* ist ‚sinnlos, zwecklos'.

point Verb. *point to something* ist ‚auf etwas hindeuten, hinweisen.' Ebenso *point out that ...* und *point out something.*
environmentalists who point to the damage done by dams
A recent study by the OECD points out that existing energy taxes in industrial countries already reduce the output of carbon dioxide.
He points out some drawbacks. Er weist auf einige Nachteile hin.

problem. *a problem* ist eine schwierige Situation, die eine Lösung braucht. Die Art des Problems wird durch Adjektive bezeichnet: *a big, common, concrete, (an) environmental, fundamental, global, political, serious, structural problem.*
Oder durch vorgestellte Substantive: *business problems, measurement problems, price-index problems, supply problems, tax problems.*
The real problem is how can America cut its budget deficit.
In Germany the problem is the opposite.
the problem of separating cause from effect
the problems of conventional discount rates
There are two problems with this.
This leaves a problem. Das birgt ein Problem.

Verb mit *problem* als Objekt: *address* ‚ansprechen', *create, deal with, highlight* ‚deutlich machen', *solve, tackle* ‚angehen'.

Siehe *problem* in GEFAHREN, PROBLEME, SCHWIERIGKEITEN.

question. *a question* ist eine Frage: *another question, a big, controversial, disturbing, further, (an) interesting, main, underlying question. a key question* ist eine Schlüsselfrage.

Die wesentlichen Konstruktionen sind in den folgenden Beispielen enthalten.
the most controversial question about Vietnam's economic future
[This] is a question for politicians.
This question is hard to answer.
The question is how/whether/when Die Frage ist, wie/ob/wann ...
the question of how this would be financed die Frage, wie dies finanziert würde

Fragen werden gestellt (*raised*), beantwortet (*answered*), ignoriert (*ignored*).

Das Verb *to question something* bedeutet ‚fragen', meist zum Zwecke des Hinterfragens oder weil ein Verdacht vorliegt.

suggest. Im Zusammenhang mit Personen, Institutionen bedeutet *suggest* ‚vorschlagen, den Vorschlag machen'. Mit anderen Subjekten ist die Bedeutung ‚nahelegen'. *suggest* wird auch mit einem *that*-Satz konstruiert, in diesem *that*-Satz werden meist Modalverben wie *will, may* usw. eingesetzt. Das *that* kann weggelassen werden.
This suggests a different approach.
The theorists suggested a modification.
[This] could suggest that future output will rise.
But history suggests that Western Europe's fears may be exaggerated.
Mr Garber suggests that this pattern has many possible explanations.

talk. *talk about* ist ‚über etwas reden, verhandeln', *talk of* ist ‚von etwas (als etwas) reden'.
Congress is talking about new trade-law initiatives.
It has become fashionable to talk of numerous capitalist 'models'.

Man kann durch Reden bewirken, dass etwas an Bedeutung/Wert zunimmt (*to talk something up*) oder abnimmt (*to talk something down*).
Officals appeared to be trying to talk the dollar down against the yen.
Zu oder mit jemandem reden ist *talk to/with someone*.

Das Substantiv *talk* wird ebenfalls durch *about* oder *of* ergänzt. *a talk* ist eine Verhandlung, ein Gespräch.
trade talks

GATT talks
trade agreement talks

AT

Die Präposition *at* wird zu verschiedenen Zwecken verwendet.

Als Ergänzung. Mit *at* werden Verben, Substantive und Adjektive ergänzt.
Or look at banking. Oder nehmen wir das Bankwesen.
A glance at corporate borrowing and commercial-property prices over the past decade ... Ein Blick auf ...
Government officials from around the world arrived at the Rocky Mountain resort.
Game theorists have been good at explaining the intricacies underlying strategic interdependence ... haben erfolgreich ... erklärt
the alarm at declining values Beunruhigung über ...

Mit Zahlen. Nach Verben, die einen Status quo oder Gleichbleiben bezeichnen, folgen auf *at* Zahlenangaben, im Sinne von ‚bei'.
Consumer-price inflation remained at 2%.
Producer-price inflation stayed at 2.3%.
... a year earlier, it stood at 7.7%.
Japan's jobless rate, at 3.0% in August, is still the lowest ...
Italy's visible-trade surplus stood at $3.3 billion in August.
the biggest external deficit, at $23 billion in 1993

Zahlen, die angeben, „zu" welchem Preis etwas verkauft wird, gehen mit *at*.
Canadians had the cheapest water, at $0.35 per cubic metre.
... by far the highest water charges, at $1.69 per cubic metre.

Nachgestelltes *at most* gibt eine Höchstsumme an.
$387m at most.

Außerdem
at a price of
at a moderate discount rate

Das Lebensalter wird mit *at* formuliert.
at the age of 21
Most workers retire at 55.

Zeitangaben. *at* entspricht meist ‚zu'.
at the same time
at the beginning of 1988
at the end of the season
at the time (when) zu der Zeit, als
at the moment, at present zur Zeit, derzeit

Ortsangaben. *at* steht als Ortsangabe ‚in' bei kleineren Städten, bei Fabriken oder Unternehmen. Ferner als ‚an, am' bei Institutionen, als ‚bei' in Bezug auf den Arbeitgeber oder eine Institution.
the tin mines at Bom Futuro
production problems at Russia's Norilsk plant
Cocoa traders at Gill & Duffus expect a world cocoa demand of ...
an economist at Brown University
at any given airport

at entspricht ‚bei, auf', wenn von (in einem weiten Sinne) sozialen Ereignissen, wie Treffen, Konferenzen, die Rede ist.
at a recent meeting of EC finance ministers
at their spring meeting in Maastricht

Rangplätze werden mit *at xth place* formuliert.
India comes in at fifth place in the league

In britischen Texten ist *at home (and abroad)* ‚im Inland (und Ausland)'.

Weitere Adverbiale
at all (in Sätzen mit Verneinung) überhaupt
at an astonishing rate mit erstaunlicher Geschwindigkeit
at best im günstigsten Fall
at first zuerst, zunächst
at last zuletzt, schließlich
at least mindestens
at once sofort
at the other extreme

BEDINGUNG, NOTWENDIGKEIT

Siehe auch den Abschnitt ERWARTEN, SCHÄTZEN, VORAUSSAGEN.

basis. Mit *basis* ‚Grundlage' (im Plural *bases* [ˈbeɪsiːz], jedoch dann meist im Sinne von ‚Stützpunkte') kann man formulieren, dass Voraussetzungen, Grundlagen bestehen.
a basis for debate and decision
a basis for trade sanctions
on the basis of a detailed comparison
on this basis, ...

case. *case* wird in einigen Wendungen gebraucht, um Voraussetzungen oder Bedingungen zu benennen.
in this particular case in diesem besonderen Fall
in the case of global pollution im Falle einer globalen Umweltverschmutzung
in the case of agriculture was die Landwirtschaft betrifft
in this case wenn das so ist
This seems to be the case.
in any case in jedem Falle, wie dem auch sei
in either case in beiden Fällen
in every case in jedem der vorliegenden Fälle
in almost every case
in each case in jedem Fall (von den vorher erwähnten)
in Japan's case im Falle Japans, was Japan betrifft
‚In jedem Fall, jedenfalls' ist *at any rate*.

condition. Mit *condition* kann man sich auf den allgemeinen Zustand von etwas beziehen.
the cost of restoring the environment to its previous condition ... in ihren früheren Zustand ...
in good condition in gutem Zustand

condition(s) kann auch ‚Bedingung(en)' bedeuten. Die Bedeutung ‚Bedingung(en)' ist wahrscheinlich bei Ergänzungen mit *of*. Sie ist vorhanden bei Ergänzungen mit *for* oder *that* sowie bei bestimmten Phrasen.
conditions of membership

a measure of whether conditions for the poorest are improving
the condition that ...
on certain conditions bei gewissen Bedingungen
under limited conditions
labour-market conditions
supply and demand conditions
monetary conditions
to meet the necessary conditions die notwendigen Bedingungen erfüllen
extreme market conditions

force Verb. *be forced* (Passivform) bedeutet, dass man unter bestimmten Umständen gezwungen ist, etwas zu tun.
Italy, Canada and Sweden are all being forced to pay bigger risk premiums.
Japan is being forced to run an excessively tight monetary policy.

Man kann auch jemanden zwingen, etwas zu tun, *force someone* (Aktivform).
It allows governments ... to force foreign producers to license local firms to use their technology.
The surge in the dollar in the first half of the 1980s – and hence stiffer foreign competition – forced manufacturers to become more efficient.

force kann auch mit Objekt und einer Adverbialbestimmung konstruiert werden.
This could force retail prices down and sales up. Dies könnte dazu führen, dass die Einzelhandelspreise fallen und der Verkauf steigt.

given. *given* wird in Nebensätzen verwendet, im Sinne von ‚wenn man bedenkt, voraussetzt, annimmt, dass'.
Given average weather, world production is expected to recover to 560m tonnes next season.
Leading indicators are hardly a precise science, given the long and variable lags.
That is hardly surprising, though, given that raw materials account for only about 10% of total production costs. Aber dies ist nicht weiter verwunderlich, wenn man bedenkt, dass ...

have to. Siehe *must* in diesem Abschnitt.

if. Die Konjunktion *if* ‚wenn, falls' wird in mehreren Satztypen verwendet.

Mit *if* kann gesagt werden: ‚wenn das eine der Fall ist, dann ist auch das andere der Fall'.

Der *if*-Satz und der Hauptsatz haben das *present tense*. Das trifft auch für *If... then...* zu. Das Miteinander der beiden erwähnten Fakten wird als zwangsläufig gesehen, das eine bedingt das andere.

If a p/e [price/earnings ratio] is above average, investors expect profits to rise.
But, ultimately, threats are not much use if there are no jobs available.
If firm X sets a high price, firm Y's best choice is to undercut it.

In diesem Typ ist auch das *present perfect* möglich (wenngleich selten).

If structural adjustment has made little difference to the lot of the poor, has it been a waste of time? Wenn die strukturellen Anpassungen wenig am Schicksal der Armen geändert haben, war dann alles Zeitverschwendung?

Wenn im *if*-Satz das *present tense* steht und im Hauptsatz ein Modalverb (wie *will, may, must, can, should*), ist die Zwangsläufigkeit des Wenn-dann geschwächt. Dann wird etwas aller Wahrscheinlichkeit nach eintreten *(will)*, es kann eintreten *(may)*, sollte der Fall sein *(should)* usw.

If the dollar is dethroned, America will lose some of the benefits of being the issuer of the leading currency.
If the jobless rate is higher than this, inflation will slow; if lower, it will accelerate.
If inflation stays low in this cycle, it will be because of better policy, not because the world is safer.
If the euro is even a modest success, there will be powerful pressures on Britain to sign up, however belatedly.
If central banks can engineer a controlled slowdown ..., then it may indeed be possible to avoid an inflationary surge.
If consumption goes up or health services improve, fewer babies should die.

Ein *if*-Satz mit *past tense* formuliert das hypothetische ‚wenn etwas der Fall wäre, dann wäre/würde (sollte, könnte) ...' Im Hauptsatz steht *would/should/could*.

If foreigners held less of their wealth in dollars, America would face higher interest rates.
Environmental lawsuits and regulatory debates would be starved of ammunition if economists did not lob their damage estimates into the fray.

In diesem Typ von *if*-Satz steht in der dritten Person Singular *were* anstelle von *was*.

If the Berle-Means model were truly the most efficient, it would continue to thrive.

Bei ‚wenn etwas der Fall gewesen wäre, dann wäre/hätte ...' steht im *if*-Satz das *past perfect* (im Beispiel: *had pegged*). Im Hauptsatz steht *would* oder ein ähnliches

Hilfsverb, gefolgt von *have* und dem Partizip Perfekt des Verbs (im Beispiel: *would have had).*
If the governments concerned had instead pegged their exchange rates to a stable currency, they would have had a more visible anchor against inflation. Wenn die betroffenen Regierungen ihre Wechselraten an eine stabile Währung gekoppelt hätten ...

Verkürzte *if*-Sätze. *if*-Sätze können zusätzlich zum *if* nur ein Adjektiv enthalten *(if possible),* vor einem Verb kann das Subjekt entfallen *(if used).*
You probably do need a leader with a vision, a strong political base and, if possible, an advanced degree in economics . ... wenn möglich ...
But amnesties run the risk of making the government look soft: if used repeatedly, they may encourage tax evaders to think that their crime carries no penalty at all. ... wenn häufig eingesetzt ...

Bei Aufzählungen oder Reihungen bedeutet *if* ‚wenngleich'. Mit *not* ist es dann ‚wenn nicht (sogar)'.
Moreover, economic policy embodies a persistent, if gentle, bias towards inflation.
Infrastructure represents, if not the engine, then the wheels, of economic activity. ... wenn nicht den Motor, dann doch die Räder ...
Even dictators pay some attention to public opinion, abroad if not at home.

Mit *if so* sagt man ‚wenn das gerade Gesagte der Fall ist', ‚wenn dem so ist'.
If so, America would have the highest inflation rate among the Group of Seven economies.
If so, even after recovery, unemployment will remain high – or inflation will pick up.

if-Sätze brauchen nicht notwendigerweise einen folgenden Hauptsatz.
If only life were that simple. Wenn das Leben nur so einfach wäre.

Das *if* kann mit anderen Konjunktionen kombiniert werden.
... because if wages are raised to attract another worker, they must be paid to all existing workers as well. ... denn wenn man höhere Löhne bietet, um ..., dann ...
Experience showed, he claimed, that if real interest rates were held below their long-term equilibrium, inflation would start to move up. Die Erfahrung zeige, behauptete er, dass, wenn ... dann ...
So if GDP fell, his income would be protected. Wenn daher/also ..., dann wäre ...
But what if the minimum wage is increased? Was, wenn ... ?
... firms would use such arrangements only if they made delivery cheaper, and consumers would benefit. ... nur dann, wenn ...
Even if they promised to do so, there would be no way of holding them to their word. Selbst/Auch (dann) wenn ...

if at all bedeutet ‚wenn überhaupt'.
How, if at all, did governments maintain the political support that made reform possible?
if steht für *whether*. *It is still not known when, or if, China will join.*
Zu *as if* siehe *as if, as though* in VERGLEICH, ÄHNLICHKEIT, UNTERSCHIED.

meet. Das Verb *meet* kann in der Bedeutung ‚(Kriterien, Bedingungen) erfüllen' verwendet werden.
Few employee share schemes meet any of these criteria.
... if Russia is willing to meet the necessary conditions.

must. *must* und *have to* bedeuten ‚es ist notwendig, dass'. *(have got to* wird in formellen Texten nicht verwendet.)
Die Entscheidung, ob *must* oder *have to* verwendet wird, ist zum Teil grammatischer Art: *must* ist ein Modalverb und kann nicht mit anderen Modalverben *(can, shall, would, will* usw.) kombiniert werden. Daher:
160m Soviet workers might have to change their jobs.
The banks would have to back them with more capital.
Therefore big borrowers will have to pay more.

must wird nicht im *past tense* verwendet. Daher:
The McKinsey team had to adjust their data ... mussten ...

must not bedeutet ‚darf/dürfen nicht'. Man sagt damit also, dass es wichtig ist, dass etwas nicht getan wird.
Governments must not help uncompetitive industries indefinitely. Die Regierungen dürfen wettbewerbsunfähige Industrien nicht für unbegrenzte Zeit unterstützen.

Will man dagegen sagen ‚es ist nicht nötig, dass etwas getan wird', verwendet man *do not have to* (oder *need not* oder *do not need to* plus Verb*)*.
Retailers with exclusive dealerships and territories do not have to compete. ... müssen nicht (unbedingt)/brauchen nicht ...

must wird verwendet, wenn etwas aufgrund von Regeln, Plänen, Gesetzen so sein muss.
... whereas under Mr Williamson's scheme, governments must shoulder that responsibility for themselves.

Mit *must* werden zu erfüllende Bedingungen, Voraussetzungen benannt.

First, the American and Japanese governments must avoid any weakening of the yen – if necessary, through foreign-exchange intervention. Second, the Japanese government must implement its various promised fiscal packages ...

Mit *have to* kann man eine abgeschwächte Notwendigkeit formulieren, also sagen, dass etwas sehr wichtig ist. Dieses *have to* ist oft begleitet von Adverbien wie *often, generally, obviously*.
An international currency has to perform several functions.
They often have to act on inadequate information.

necessary, necessarily. Das Adjektiv ist *necessary* ‚nötig, notwendig', das Adverb *necessarily* ‚notwendigerweise'.
Exchange-rate changes are a necessary part of the adjustment process.
A strong GATT is necessary.
to meet the necessary conditions
It is necessary to distinguish between ... Man muss ...

Das Konzept ‚es ist (nicht) notwendigerweise so, dass' wird durch *not necessarily* ausgedrückt.
But faster growth does not necessarily mean higher inflation.
... probably (though not necessarily) ...

need Verb. *need* gehört zu verschiedenen Verbtypen und hat verschiedene Konstruktionen.
In der Konstruktion *somebody needs something* bedeutet es ‚brauchen, haben müssen, erforderlich sein für'. Die verneinte Form wird mit *do* und *not* gebildet.
You probably do need a leader with a vision.
You don't need a dictator or a crisis.
East German firms will need much more capital equipment.
those who need the most help
Governments will need more fiscal flexibility ...

Mit *need* plus Verb-*ing* wird gesagt, dass etwas getan werden muss.
GDP needs adjusting.
Creditors ... need convincing that ... Die Gläubiger müssen davon überzeugt werden, dass ...

Wenn *need* mit einem Infinitiv kombiniert wird, dann mit einem *to*-Infinitiv: ‚es ist erforderlich, dass'.
Emerging economies need to invest heavily in infrastructure.

Economics needs to take psychology more seriously.
These links need to be preserved.

Die Kombination *need* plus Verb kann, im Präsens, auf zweierlei Weise verneint werden: mit *need + not +* Verb oder mit *do + not + need + to +* Verb. Im *past tense* steht die *do-*Verneinung.
The regional approach need not cause a trade war.
Productivity gaps do not need to be closed entirely.
[They] did not need to worry about popular resentment. ... brauchten nicht/mussten nicht ....

Eine Konstruktion wie **Firms do not need invest more* ist nicht möglich, ebenso nicht **Firms need not to invest more.*
In der Konstruktion *need + not +* Verb ist *need* ein Modalverb, daher fehlt das *-s* in der 3. Person Präsens Singular.
But that need not rule out a short-term stimulus ...

need Substantiv. ‚Es ist nicht erforderlich, dass/es braucht nicht ...' kann mit *need* konstruiert werden (und anschließendem *for* plus Substantiv oder *to* plus Verb).
There is no need for a repeat of the deflationary 1930s.
There may be no need to panic.

Auch sonst geht *need* ‚Bedürfnis, Erfordernis' mit *for* plus Substantiv bzw. *to* plus Verb.
the need for a more flexible wage structure
the need to bring wage inflation down
There was the usual fretting about the need for any aid to be accompanied by a credible economic-reform programme. ... Diskussion ... darüber, ob es erforderlich sei, dass jede Hilfe von einem tragfähigen Wirtschaftsreformprogramm begleitet sein müsse.
The need for the government to guarantee, in one way or another, the integrity of the banking system goes virtually unchallenged.
needs sind die Bedürfnisse.
the increased financing needs of Eastern Europe
the varied needs of firms and shareholders

provided. Mit *provided* wird eine Voraussetzung (als Nebensatz) eingeführt. Falls das Subjekt nicht unmittelbar auf *provided* folgt, wird *that* eingefügt.
... provided the official believes that he is likely to be in his job for some time.

... vorausgesetzt, der Angestellte glaubt, er werde wahrscheinlich länger auf dieser Stelle sein.
Poorer countries are right to place a lower value on safety – provided they use the correct method to do so.
... provided that on average they still comply with the RPI-minus-x formula.

once. *once* wird als Adverb gebraucht („einmal"; weitere Konstruktionen sind *once again* „wieder einmal", *once more* „einmal mehr") – aber auch als Konjunktion im Sinne von „wenn erst einmal ... dann".
However, evidence shows that, once people have been out of work for more than a year or so, they can easily be lost from the workforce for ever. ... wenn Menschen erst einmal mehr als ca. ein Jahr arbeitslos sind, dann ...
In Europe, once a worker has lost his job such mechanisms keep him jobless.
So once the initial costly work has been done, most of these ideas become very cheap to copy. Wenn daher erst einmal die anfängliche und kostspielige Arbeit getan ist, dann ...
Once built, power stations and roads cannot be moved or put to other uses. Wenn sie erst einmal errichtet sind, können Kraftwerke und Straßen nicht ...

require. *require* „ist verlangen, erforderlich sein".
That requires cuts in the huge budget.
They should require yes-or-no answers.

„Von jemandem verlangen, dass etwas getan wird" ist *require* plus Substantiv plus *to* plus Verb. (Hierfür im Passiv auch eine Konstruktion mit *for*.)
The Federal Reserve Bank Act of 1978 requires the Fed to pursue full employment as well as low inflation.
Countries should be required to reduce budget deficits.
Then some substantial amount of revenue will be required for the good to be sold at all.

require kann mit einem *that*-Satz konstruiert werden.
... achieving such a rate in the meantime will require that both macroeconomic management and the succession to Deng Xiaoping go smoothly.

requirement. *a requirement* bezeichnet eine Voraussetzung oder Bedingung *(for something)*.
entry requirements for EMU

requirement kann mit einem *that*-Satz erweitert werden.
These included the requirement that the machinery would be used to make products that met performance targets. ... die Bedingung, dass die Maschinen so eingesetzt würden, dass ...

unless. Mit der Konjunktion *unless* wird ‚es sei denn, dass' ausgedrückt, oder ‚vorausgesetzt, dass' oder ‚wenn ... nicht'.
China will be kept out of the club unless it signs the TRIPs agreement and complies with it within a year, say the Americans.
But such sharing will be a rarity unless firms think that their ideas are safe from the copiers. ... vorausgesetzt, die Firmen glauben ...
Economic theory argues that unless wages reflect productivity and skill differences, firms will have little incentive to hire low-skilled workers.
Unless productivity grows, living standards stagnate. Wenn die Produktivität nicht steigt ...
... *unless supply and demand conditions change dramatically.* ... es sei denn, die Bedingungen von Angebot und Nachfrage ändern sich erheblich.

when. *when* (als Adverb und als Konjunktion) drückt eine Zeitangabe aus, keine Bedingung. Siehe *when* in ZEIT, dort in „2.4 Gleichzeitigkeit".

BELOW – UNDER

Als Adverb. Das Adverb *below* steht unmittelbar nach einem Substantiv, im Sinne von ‚im Text nachfolgend, untenstehend'.
As the table below shows ... wie die nachfolgende Tabelle zeigt ...
the chart below die folgende Graphik
about which more below davon unten mehr

Als Präposition (mit Zahl).
Sowohl *below* als auch *under* können mit Zahlen verbunden werden, im Sinne von ‚unter, weniger als'.
a discount rate of under 10%
just under 50% of GDP
Annualised inflation is now below 10%.

Dabei wird *under* häufig zusammen mit ‚geringfügig' gesetzt: *just under, a bit under, slightly under.*

Für ‚jünger als' steht *under* plus Zahl.
the population aged under 15 and over 64
23% of French under 25-year-olds

Als Präposition (mit Substantiven). *below* wird verwendet, wenn es sich um Angaben handelt, die „unter" einem bestimmten Niveau oder einer bestimmten Grenze liegen. Substantive nach *below* sind daher häufig *level, target, rate, peak, costs.*
A limit that should be well below current levels.
That was far below the Fed's target.
below the poverty line unterhalb der Armutsgrenze
for prices far below what they had offered

Das ‚unter' in diesem Sinne (‚unterhalb einer Grenze usw.') wird nicht durch *under* realisiert.

Mit *under* werden einige Typen von Adverbialen konstruiert. *under* steht für ‚unter, gemäß, entsprechend' in Verbindung mit Regelungen, Plänen, Methoden, Rahmenbedingungen.
under its current law
under one method
under existing GATT rules
under the American model
under their proposed scheme
under trade treaties
under pessimistic assumptions

Ähnlich ‚unter' im Sinne von ‚unter der Herrschaft, Regierung von'.
under the Tory government
Russia under the communists
under the existing tax regime

under führt auch negative Begleitumstände ein, besonders ‚Druck, Drohung'.
under pressure from America
under the threat of imminent disaster
This traditional view is coming under attack.
Brazil refused to negotiate under duress.
The ERM has come under strain for several reasons.

Entwicklungen oder Zustände, die *under control* sind, hat man im Griff. Entwicklungen, die im Gange sind, sind *under way*.
with recovery already well under way

BÖRSE

Die Börsen (wie etwa die in Frankfurt, London, New York) werden als *stock markets,* auch *stockmarkets,* bezeichnet, im Textzusammenhang auch als *markets,* ferner als *stock exchanges,* seltener als *bourses* [bʊəsɪz].

Die wichtigsten Börsen sind *Bangkok* [bæŋˈkɒk], *Brussels* [ˈbrʌsəlz], *Buenos Aires* [ˌbweɪnɒsˈaɪərez], *Copenhagen* [ˌkəʊpənˈheɪgn], *Frankfurt, Hong Kong* [ˌhɒŋˈkɒŋ], *Johannesburg* [dʒəʊˈhænɪsbɜːg], *Kuala Lumpur* [ˌkwɑːləˈlʊmpʊə], *London* [ˈlʌndən], *Lusaka* [luːˈsɑːkə], *Madrid* [məˈdrɪd], *Mexico City* [ˌmeksɪkəʊˈsɪti], *Milan* [mɪˈlæn], *Moscow* [ˈmɒskəʊ], *New York* [ˌnjuːˈjɔːk], *Paris* [ˈpærɪs], *Prague* [prɑːg], *Sao Paulo* [saʊmˈpaʊləʊ], *Shanghai* [ˌʃæŋˈhaɪ], *Stockholm* [ˈstɒkhəʊm], *Sydney* [ˈsɪdni], *Taipei* [ˌtaɪˈpeɪ], *Wall Street* [ˈwɔːlstriːt] (= *New York*), *Warsaw* [ˈwɔːsɔː], *Zurich* [ˈzjʊərɪk].

Die Börsen in Asien sind die *Asian markets,* die in Südamerika *Latin American markets,* die in Europa *European markets.*
Most Asian stock markets fell this week.

emerging stockmarkets sind Börsen in den sog. Schwellenländern.

Eine Börse hat einen Aktienpreisindex (*stock price index,* im Plural *stock prices indices* [ˈstɒk praɪsɪz ˈɪndɪsiːz]). An der New Yorker Börse ist dies der *Dow Jones Index* [ˌdaʊ dʒəʊnz ˈɪndeks], an der Londoner Börse der *Financial Times Share Index FTSI* – die sogenannten *business barometers.*

Der jährliche Höchst- bzw. Tiefstand ist das *high* bzw. *low (for the year).* Der absolute Höchststand ist das *record high.* Änderungen in Prozent (*% change*) ergeben sich z.B. im Vergleich (*on*) zur Vorwoche (*on the week*).
Wall Street ended 3.9% up on a week earlier.

Das Verhalten von Börsen und die Situationen werden oft so beschrieben, als handele es sich um Personen.
[This] seemed not to trouble Wall Street, which finished up 1.6%.
Most stockmarkets were in a cheerier mood this week. freundlicher
[This] left stockmarkets depressed.
Fears of higher interest rates depressed most markets.

Bourses had a mixed week.
The stockmarkets in our table had a bad week.
Most bourses lost more ground this week.
Wall Street remained nervous.
[This] sent jitters through the Tokyo market. ... versetzte Tokio in helle Aufregung
There was a buoyant mood ... Es herrschte Hochstimmung ...
Wall Street ended the week 0.1% lower.

Wenn solche Stimmungen begründet werden, dann oft mit der Präposition *on:*
on fears of
on worries that
on hopes that

Bei steigenden Kursen spricht man von *bullish markets,* der Zustand ist *bullishness,* Käufer, die darauf setzen, sind sog. *bulls* und verhalten sich *bullish (about something).*
Our seers are more bullish this month about America and Britain: they have revised their growth forecasts for 1994 up by 0.2 percentage points.

Bei fallenden Kursen ist der Markt *bearish* (das Substantiv lautet *bearishness*). Eine stagnierende, lustlose Börse wird als *sluggish* bezeichnet.

Zahlenangaben beim Steigen oder Fallen beziehen sich entweder auf Prozente (*percent*) oder Punkte (*points*).
Both Frankfurt and Milan dropped by more than 3%.
Wall Street fell by 91 points on November 22nd.

Aufwärtsbewegungen.
Hong Kong also hit record highs.
New York reached an all-time high. ... einen absoluten Höchststand.
Eight other markets hit record peaks during the week.
The Dow pushed through the 8,000 barrier. ... durchbrach die Grenze von 8000 Punkten.
Milan was the star, ...
Sydney had its largest one-day rise. ... an einem Tag ...
The markets in our table rallied this week. ... erholten sich schnell.
Madrid rose 4.8%.
Wall Street gained 0.5%.
Tokyo jumped by 2.5%. ... sprang auf ...
Milan led the way ... ... führte die Entwicklung an ...
... climbing by 3.6%
Wall Street edged up by 0.2%. ... zog um 0,2% an.

New York's strong showing. ... starke Vorstellung
Taipei was the exception.
Warsaw was this week's star.
... gaining 4.8%

Abwärtsbewegungen.
The world stockmarket index fell by 0.3%.
Both Frankfurt and Milan dropped by more than 3%. ... fielen um mehr als 3%.
Four (Brussels, Copenhagen, Paris and Vienna) sank to new lows for the year.
... sanken auf einen neuen Jahrestiefstand.
Sydney hit a new low for the year.
Hong Kong touched a new low for the year.
London slipped on fears of big rights issues. ... glitt aufgrund von Befürchtungen ab ...
But Tokyo tumbled 7.6% on fears of a new political scandal ... ... stürzte um 7,6% ab ...
Tokyo had its worst one-day loss of 1998. ... den höchsten Verlust während eines Tages
Madrid lost 2.0%.
Wall Street fell by 91 points on November 22nd.
Frankfurt declined by 1.7%. ... ging zurück ...
The market finished the week 0.3% up. ... 0.3% höher ...
Tokyo fell by 1%.
London fell 1.8%.
Tokyo slumped by 2.4%. ... brach um 2,4% ein.
Frankfurt suffered the most, plunging by 5.3%. ... mit einem plötzlichen Kurssturz von 5,3%.
London finished 2.7% lower. ... 2,7% niedriger.
Wall Street was still 1.1% down on the week. ... lag immer noch 1,1% niedriger als in der Vorwoche.
The biggest faller was Madrid, which shed 1.3%. ... das um 1,3% nach- bzw. abgab.
... the continuing weakness of bond prices took most markets down.
The worst performer, however, was Milan ...
Latin American markets lost ground.
Share prices fell across the board this week. ... fielen allgemein

Gelegentlich tritt die Präposition *bar* auf:
bar Tokyo mit Ausnahme von Tokio.

Siehe auch den Abschnitt STEIGEN, MEHR WERDEN ...

BUSINESS

business ['bɪznɪs] wird in verschiedenen Bedeutungen verwendet.
Wenn etwas *somebody's business* ist oder *the business of ...*, dann ist es Sache, Angelegenheit von jemandem/etwas, fällt also in eine bestimmte Zuständigkeit. (In dieser Bedeutung nur im Singular.)
Although damage at home is mostly the business of the polluting country, damage to a planetary resource, such as the ozone layer, or a local resource, such as the sea, is also other people's business.

a ... business (for someone) – meist mit einem Adjektiv, das Schwierigkeiten oder Komplikationen ausdrückt – stellt jemanden vor Probleme. (In dieser Bedeutung nur im Singular.)
... but accurate price-setting is a tough business. ... ist ein Problem, eine schwierige Sache, eine harte Nuss.
a puzzling business for economists
Comparing productivity across borders is a hazardous business. ... ein gefährliches Unterfangen.

Ebenfalls nur im Singular (und ohne den unbestimmten Artikel *a*) steht *business* für ‚Arbeit, die zu tun ist'.
plenty of unfinished business for governments

Mit entsprechenden Substantiven davor bedeutet *business* ‚-gewerbe, -branche, -zweig', im Plural dann *businesses* ['bɪznɪsɪz].
The third service sector McKinsey examined was the television, film and video business.
Yet look closer at Sony: as much as a fifth of its revenues now come from its film and music businesses.

Weitere Kombinationen: *airline business, property business, telephone business, fast-food business, energy business, non-farming businesses, banking business.*

business (im Singular) kann ‚Umsatz' bedeuten.
Service activities probably account for at least half of Sony's business.

Jede Person, Firma, Gesellschaft, die mit Absicht auf Gewinn etwas herstellt, verkauft oder Dienstleistungen erbringt, kann als *business* (im Plural *businesses*) bezeichnet werden.
an entrepreneur wishing to open a business in Russia

‚Geschäftsbeziehungen mit' werden als *business (with)* bezeichnet, *business* nur im Singular, ohne den bestimmten Artikel.
Business with Hong Kong contracted slightly.

business (im Singular, ohne den unbestimmten Artikel *a*) kann die Wirtschaft, die allgemeine Wirtschaftslage, auch den Handel allgemein, bezeichnen.
business confidence Konjunkturoptimismus, konjunkturelle Zuversicht
business cycle Konjunkturzyklus, -verlauf
London Business School
Harvard Business School
business economists
the business world
productivity in the business sector ... in der Privatwirtschaft
international business
business investment

the study of business administration Betriebswirtschaftslehre.

Hinweis. Es ist nicht der Fall, dass *business* generell mit „Geschäft" zu übersetzen ist, wie auch Geschäft nicht generell mit „*business*" zu übersetzen ist. Die Konsultation größerer Wirtschaftswörterbücher wird empfohlen.

BUT

Siehe auch *but* in GEGENSATZ, EINRÄUMUNG.

Die Konstruktionen *all but* und *anything but* haben eine besondere Bedeutung.

all but in Verbindung mit Substantiven ist ‚alle außer'.
all but four countries alle außer vier Ländern/Staaten
After last week's falls, all but three of the stockmarkets in our table rose this week. [Drei sind wieder gefallen, alle anderen gestiegen.]

all but mit Adjektiven oder Adverbien besagt, dass etwas fast oder nahezu der Fall ist.
Their problems are all but over. ... so gut wie überstanden.

anything but mit Adjektiv bedeutet, dass etwas nicht der Fall ist.
However, success is anything but assured. ... alles andere als garantiert/durchaus nicht garantiert.
In other words, trade in these industries is anything but 'free'. ... alles andere als „frei".

BUY – PURCHASE – SELL – SALE

buy, bought, bought. Was gekauft werden kann, *can be bought*. Das *buy* kann für sich alleine stehen, mit einem Objekt und/oder der Angabe von wem man etwas kauft (*from*).
the right to buy
buying local currency
Consumers had decided not to buy the drug.
In many cases these firms buy from fellow group members.
When a customer buys a car from a car maker...
Man kauft etwas *at the price of...* oder *for $10,000*. ‚Im Wert von' wird so formuliert: *buying $235 billion-worth of goods.*

buy off bedeutet, dass man jemandem Geld zahlt, um Nachteile zu vermeiden.
a way of buying off opponents

buy out someone: Ein Partner kauft den Teil, den der andere vorher gehalten hat. Hierzu das Substantiv *a buy-out.* Das Sich-Einkaufen ist *buying-in.*

buyers sind Käufer, Kunden, wie in *buyers and sellers, potential buyers, house-buyer, home-buyer,* aber auch die Einkäufer von Firmen, die fertige Produkte oder Materialien kaufen.

purchase. *purchase* ist ein formelles Wort für ‚kaufen'. Das Substantiv *purchase* ist die Tätigkeit des Kaufens oder der Gegenstand des Kaufs. *the purchasers* sind die Käufer. *the purchasing power* ist die Kaufkraft einer Währung, eines Landes, einer Gruppe. *purchase(s)* wird am häufigsten verwendet, wenn vom Kauf von Geld oder Wertpapieren die Rede ist.
domestic purchases of foreign securities Inlandskäufe ausländischer Wertpapiere
official purchases of US equity and bonds

sale. Mit *sale/sales* wird ‚Verkauf/Verkäufe' bezeichnet. Der Verkauf von etwas ist *sale/sales of something,* durch jemanden *by someone,* an jemanden *to someone.*
sales of colour televisions
sales of new products
sales by the Bank of Japan
sales by American firms to American subsidiaries

Der Plural *sales (of a product)* bezeichnet die Menge der von einer Firma oder in einem Gebiet verkauften Waren, aber auch verschiedene „Vorfälle des Verkaufens": *the sale of a house/the sales of houses.*
Das Objekt des Verkaufens kann vorgestellt werden.
asset sales
new-car sales
dollar sales

retail sales ist der Einzelhandelsumsatz, *retail sale* der Ladenverkauf.
Beachte, dass in vielen Verbindungen als erstes Element *sales* (und nicht nur *sale*) steht:
sales activity
sales agreement
sales campaign
sales company Vertriebsgesellschaft

Doch: *sale contract, sale price.*

Etwas, das *on sale* ist, ist vorrätig, oft als Sonderangebot; etwas, das *for sale* ist, wird, meist von Privatpersonen, zum Kauf angeboten.

sell, sold, sold. *sell* kann für sich, ohne Objekt, stehen.
a further reason for selling ein weiterer Grund für den Verkauf

something sells (meist mit Ergänzungen wie *well*) bedeutet ‚etwas verkauft sich (gut), wird gekauft.'
[During the 17th century] rare bulbs sold for a fortune. ...konnte man seltene Tulpenzwiebeln für ein Vermögen verkaufen.

sell wird mit Objekt konstruiert, anschließend kann der Käufer mit *to* eingeführt werden. Das Objekt muss nicht stehen.
selling oil-exploitation rights
to sell television sets
... when Pan AM sold its Heathrow services to United Airlines...
It is often inefficient to sell to entirely independent retailers.

Es wird *at the price of* ... oder *for $10,000* verkauft.
Das Partizip *sold* wird nachgestellt: *the goods sold.*

the seller ist der Verkäufer, in den meisten Fällen der von Wertpapieren.

BY

Die Präposition *by* wird zu verschiedenen Zwecken verwendet: zur Bildung des Passivs, zur Bezeichnung der Urheberschaft (*a study by Ronald Nashe*), vor Zeitangaben (siehe *by* in ZEIT, dort in „3. Präpositionen und Konjunktionen"), vor Zahlen (siehe den „Hinweis: Verben und Ergänzungen" in STEIGEN, MEHR WERDEN ...).

Mit *by* plus der *-ing*-Form eines Verbs wird ausgedrückt ‚indem das geschieht/dadurch, dass etwas geschieht/durch ...'
A monopolist might try to keep a would-be rival out of its market by threatening a price war if the rival steps in. ... indem er mit einem Preiskrieg droht, falls ...
National competition policies could be improved by making them subject to international trade rules. ... indem man sie ...
The old idea that governments could reduce unemployment by tolerating just a little more inflation – is more or less dead. ... durch Hinnahme von ...
In a new paper, William Nordhaus of Yale University starts by asking what may seem a dull question.

CAN – COULD – BE ABLE TO

Hier werden nur die Verwendungen besprochen, die für Wirtschaftstexte wichtig sind.
Siehe auch den Abschnitt *MAY – MIGHT*.

can. *can* wird als [kən] ausgesprochen – also nicht mit einem ä-Laut –, es sei denn, es wird besonders betont.
can drückt aus, dass eine bestimmte Möglichkeit gegeben ist.
Die Möglichkeit kann darin liegen, dass die Sache eben so ist, wie sie ist. In solchen Fällen muss im Deutschen nicht unbedingt das Verb ‚können' stehen.
... but trends can change aber Trends/Entwicklungen können sich auch verändern/ ... verändern sich auch.
But prices can stabilise only if monetary and fiscal policies are tight.
Die Möglichkeit, dass etwas der Fall ist oder getan werden kann, kann an den speziellen Umständen liegen oder daran, dass Personen oder Institutionen zu etwas in der

Lage bzw. fähig sind. So gesehen, ist das *can* mehrdeutig, wie das deutsche ‚können' auch.

Bei *Manufacturers can impose quality standards* muss daher der Kontext entscheiden, ob das Einführen von Qualitätsstandards „ihre Sache" ist (‚fähig zu') oder eine Möglichkeit aufgrund der Umstände. Mit *can* wird daher sowohl ‚es ist möglich, dass' formuliert als auch ‚es ist jemandem möglich ... zu.'
Americans, Britons and New Zealanders can choose their telephone company.
This hurdle can be overcome. Diese Hürde kann genommen werden.
Heavy government borrowing can be bad.

In formellen Texten ist die Verneinung *cannot* (also nicht *can't*).
Poor people cannot save much, so poor countries cannot finance the investment that is needed for them to grow.

could. Die häufigste Verwendung von *could* ist ‚jetzt oder in Zukunft ist es möglich, dass'. Diese Bedeutung verbindet sich oft mit zusätzlichen Wörtern wie *also, certainly, easily, eventually* ‚schließlich', *hardly, presumably*. Oder mit Bedingungen und Voraussetzungen.
Falling consumer prices could certainly prolong Japan's downturn.
The list could be extended indefinitely. ... könnte endlos erweitert werden.
This could force retail prices down and sales up.
It is hard to see how New York could retain its role as the world's financial capital if the dollar lost its leading role as a reserve currency. ... wie New York seine Rolle als Finanzhauptstadt beibehalten könnte, wenn ...
On average, 50% of income in developing countries is held by the richest 20% of the population. These rich elites could save more.
His analysis suggests that Britain's unemployment could be cut by 22%. ... um 22% reduziert werden könnte.
It seems unlikely that such lags could have been sustained for so long.

could bedeutet ‚konnte(n), war(en) in der Lage', wenn der Kontext klar macht, dass von Vergangenem die Rede ist.
Road freight was substantially, but not completely, liberalised by laws including the Motor Carrier Reform Act of 1980; henceforth, operators could set their own rates.
... und ab diesem Zeitpunkt konnten die Firmen die Preise diktieren.

In abhängiger Rede mit einem Verb des Sagens in der Vergangenheitsform kann *could* alle Bedeutungen haben, die auch *can* hat. Wenn also z.B. gesagt wurde *World demand can be satisfied by 10 or 15 machines*, dann lautet der Satz in abhängiger Rede:

In 1949 the boss of IBM said the firm should have nothing to do with computers, because world demand could be satisfied by 10 or 15 machines. ... könne befriedigt werden.

Mit *could have* und Partizip Perfekt wird ausgedrückt, dass eine Möglichkeit gegeben war, jetzt aber nicht mehr existiert.
Many of these problems could have been avoided. ... hätten vermieden werden können.

be able to. *be able to do something* bedeutet, dass jemand in der Lage und fähig ist, etwas zu tun, etwas tun kann. Man verwendet es vor allem, wenn von der Konstruktion das *can* nicht gesetzt werden kann.
There is the advantage of being able to trade and borrow in domestic currency.
Companies are more willing and able to borrow than they were. ... eher willens und in der Lage ...
And people would become wealthier, and so able to spend more.

be able to steht besonders dann, wenn andere Hilfsverben eingesetzt werden (und Formen wie *should can, *will can sind ja nicht möglich).
A more efficient global capital market should be better able to match savings in the developed world.
They have been able to keep stable exchange rates and control the money supply.
America may well be able to impose its will.
America's richest citizens may not be able to avoid Mr Clinton's backdated taxes.
Banks must be able to weed out bad projects.
Whether they will be able to overtake them, however, is much harder to say.

Wenn man sagt *People were able to do something*, dann impliziert das, dass sie es auch getan haben. (Anders als bei *could*.)

CAPITAL

In Texten zu Finanz und Wirtschaft wird *capital* nur im Sinne von ‚größere Geldsumme (zum Zweck des Investierens)' verwendet. Grammatisch ist *capital* „nicht zählbar", das heißt, die Pluralform *capitals existiert nicht.
capital wird nur selten für sich alleine verwendet, in der Regel steht *capital* vor einem oder mehreren Substantiven oder es werden Substantive oder Adjektive vorangestellt.

Die so entstehenden Fügungen werden anders betont als die Zusammensetzungen mit Kapital- oder -kapital im Deutschen.

Kapit**a**lkosten *c**a**pital c**o**sts*
Kapit**a**lexport *c**a**pital **e**xports;*
*st**e**rling c**a**pital*

capital ...
capital account Kapitalkonto
capital account figures
capital assets Anlagevermögen
capital control Kapitalsteuerung
capital costs Kapitalaufwand
capital equipment Kapitalausstattung
capital expenditure Kapitalaufwand
capital expenditure figures
capital exports
capital flight Kapitalflucht
capital flow Kapitalstrom
capital formation Kapitalbildung
capital gains Vermögens-, Veräußerungsgewinne
capital goods Kapitalgüter
capital goods sector Investitionsgüterbereich
capital inflow Kapitalzufluss
capital investment (langfristiges) Investitionskapital
capital issue Effektenemission
capital market Kapitalmarkt
capital markets external surpluses and deficits
capital outflow Kapitalabfluss
capital stock Aktien-, Grund-, Stammkapital
capital shortage Kapitalknappheit
capital spending Kapitalaufwand
capital surplus Kapitalüberschuss

... capital
domestic capital Inlandskapital
foreign capital ausländisches Kapital
long-term capital langfristiges Kapital
flight capital Fluchtkapital

private capital Privatvermögen
gross domestic capital investment Bruttoinlandsinvestitionen

Substantiv + Präposition + *capital*. Statt z.B. *capital imports* kann man auch, wenn es der Satzzusammenhang erfordert, *import of capital* sagen. Dabei ist der Gebrauch der Präpositionen zu berücksichtigen.

orders for capital and consumer goods
demand for capital goods
growth in capital expenditure
increase in capital expenditure
trade in capital goods
imports of capital
revision of capital expenditure
measure of capital flight
composition of capital flows
attraction of capital gains
the cost of capital
sources of capital
return on capital
revisions to capital expenditure

ECONOMIC, ECONOMICS, ECONOMIST, ECONOMY

economic Adjektiv. *economic* [ˈiːkəˈnɒmɪk] ist, von der Bedeutung her, Adjektiv sowohl für *economics* als auch für *economy*. Das Adjektiv *economical* bedeutet ‚sparsam (umgehend)'. Wird *economic* aber als Adverb verwendet (‚wirtschaftlich, wirtschaftlich gesehen/in wirtschaftlicher Hinsicht'), dann lautet die Form *economically*.
This is economically absurd.

Die meisten Vorgänge, Zustände usw., die im Deutschen mit ‚Wirtschafts-' formuliert werden, werden mit *economic* bezeichnet. Außerdem lässt sich *economic* auch mit ‚Konjunktur-' übersetzen.
economic activity/activities

economic adviser/advice
economic aid
economic benefits wirtschaftliche Vorteile
economic boom
economic choices Entscheidungen in Bezug auf die Wirtschaft
economic conditions wirtschaftliche Bedingungen
economic cycle Konjunkturzyklus
economic growth
economic indicators Konjunkturindikatoren
economic model
economic performance
economic policy Wirtschaftspolitik
economic studies
economic statistics
economic theory volkswirtschaftliche Theorie

economics. *economics* [ˈiːkəˈnɒmɪks] ist ‚Wirtschaftswissenschaft(en), Volkswirtschaft', *economics* ist Singular.

a professor of economics
the London School of Economics
the Kiel Institute of World Economics

Die einzelnen Unterdisziplinen können durch vorangestellte Adjektive oder Substantive bezeichnet werden.
monetary economics Geldtheorie
international economics
development economics
transport economics
market economics
financial economics Finanzökonomie
industrial economics

economy. Wenn man von *the economy* [ɪˈkɒnəmi] eines Landes spricht, meint man damit ‚die Wirtschaft, das Wirtschaftssystem' in diesem Land. Das Substantiv ist grammatisch „zählbar", das heißt, im Singular steht *a/the* (oder *any*, *each* usw.). (Das Wort *economy* ohne Artikel bedeutet ‚Sparsamkeit, sparsames Wirtschaften' und hat keine Pluralform.) Das jeweilige Land wird mit der -*'s*-Form oder dem entsprechenden Adjektiv gekennzeichnet.

America's economy took off like a rocket.
The American economy is set to boom.
East Asian economies
The German economy continues to slow.

Wenn von einer bestimmten Art von *economy* die Rede ist, wird das meist durch Adjektive ausgedrückt.

the global economy Weltwirtschaft
industrial economy Industriewirtschaft
a monopolized economy
a national economy Volkswirtschaft
centrally planned economy Planwirtschaft
a socialist economy
a free market economy freie Marktwirtschaft

Voranstellung anderer Substantive kommt vor, ist aber selten.

command economy Kommandowirtschaft
market economy Marktwirtschaft
East Asian miracle economies
the G7 economies/the Group of Seven economies

Übliche Adjektive (außer den oben bereits genannten) sind *big, developing, domestic* (‚Binnen-'), *emerging* (aufstrebende Schwellen-Wirtschaften), *communist, fast-growing, healthy, inflationary, international, larger, modern, poor, productive, rich, socialist, strong.*

political economy ist ‚Volkswirtschaft/Nationalökonomie' (nur im Singular, ohne *a/the*). *black economy* ist die Schattenwirtschaft.

Das Wort *economy* im Sinne von ‚Wirtschaft(ssystem)' wird vor anderen Substantiven kaum gebraucht, eine Wirtschaftstheorie ist nicht **an economy theory*. Siehe *economic* in diesem Abschnitt. Ausdrücke wie *economy* plus Substantiv bezeichnen etwas Sparsames, Billiges: *economy car, economy class.*

Von *economies* kann man sagen, *they boom, break down, develop, grow, pick up, recover, slow.*

economist. *an economist* [ɪˈkɒnəmɪst] ist ein Volkswirtschaftler oder Wissenschaftler, der mit der Wirtschaft zu tun hat. Ein *business economist* ist jemand, der für eine Firma usw. die Entwicklung der Preise, Märkte ermittelt.

ERWARTEN, SCHÄTZEN, VORAUSSAGEN

Siehe hierzu auch ZEIT, dort „2.3 Zukunft" sowie die Abschnitte WISSENSCHAFT UND FORSCHUNG und PLANEN, BEABSICHTIGEN.
Zu den Modalverben *can/could, may/might, should, will/would* siehe die entsprechenden Abschnitte CAN – COULD – BE ABLE TO; MAY – MIGHT; SHOULD – OUGHT TO sowie WILL – WOULD.

Vorbemerkung. In diesem Abschnitt wird eine Reihe von transitiven Verben (wie *assume, expect, forecast*) behandelt. Diese Verben werden oft in Passivformen (ohne folgendes *by*) verwendet. Diese Passivkonstruktion ermöglicht, dass die Vorhersage, Schätzung usw. die entsprechenden Personen bzw. Institutionen als Träger des Geschehens nicht zu nennen braucht.

appear. Gelegentlich wird *appear* im Sinne von ,in Erscheinung treten, vorkommen' verwendet.
[Several] economic studies have appeared in recent months.

Wenn nach dem *appear* ein Adjektiv steht oder ein *that*-Satz oder ein Infinitiv mit *to*, bedeutet *appear* ,den Anschein haben, als ...'
America now appears to be slowly recovering.
It appears that the model worked better when nobody was using it.

assume. *assume* ist ,glauben/setzen, dass etwas der Fall ist'. Es wird mit direktem Objekt konstruiert oder mit einem *that*-Satz, bei dem das *that* auch weggelassen werden kann. Die Konstruktion mit *that* ist die häufigste. Man kann auch *assume something to be somehow* konstruieren.
the climatic change that most studies assume   annehmen, ... von dem ... ausgehen
Until game theory came along most economists assumed that firms could ignore the effects of their behaviour on the actions of others.
Most economists assumed all firms responded in much the same way.
The stock market assumes them to be so.

Das Verb wird häufig im Passiv verwendet (ohne folgendes *by*).
It was assumed that ...
It is assumed that ...

Gleichfalls häufig sind Imperativformen und *-ing*-Formen.
Assume an oil shock.
Assume that governments believe ...   Nehmen wir an, die Regierungen glauben ...

Assuming a further increase
Assuming that governments do nothing Angenommen, ...
to assume control ist ‚Kontrolle, Herrschaft übernehmen bzw. ergreifen'.

assumption. *an assumption* ist eine Annahme, Voraussetzung. Das Wort wird mit *about* bzw. einem *that*-Satz konstruiert.
If these assumptions are correct ...
based on managers' assumptions about the future
the simplifying assumptions that the rate of interest and the wage and price levels are constant
On these assumptions, figures 1 and 2 make sense. Unter diesen Voraussetzungen/ wenn man das annimmt ...

belief. *a belief* ist eine Ansicht, Annahme.
This belief is not as silly as it seems.
grounds for belief that living standards are suppressed by policy, not poverty
Contrary to popular belief ... im Gegensatz zur allgemeinen Ansicht
... the belief that the euro is doomed to permanent weakness

believe. *believe something* ist ‚glauben, auf etwas vertrauen'.
But would it be right to believe the answer?

believe in something ist ‚glauben an, Anhänger sein von'. Es wird meist ironisch gebraucht.
She believes in GATT and all that.
a believer in free trade ein Anhänger des Freihandels

Mit der Konstruktion *believe* plus *that*-Satz wird eine Ansicht ausgedrückt. Ein *will* im *that*-Satz macht daraus eine Voraussage. Das *that* kann ausgelassen werden.
The OECD believes that this slowdown will be enough to prevent a sharp pick-up in inflation.
Most governments now believe self-employment is something to be promoted in speeches and encouraged with taxpayers' money.
The number of businessmen who believe sales will rise in the fourth quarter of 1994 now exceeds the number who believe they will fall in all of the 15 countries in our chart.
He believes the exchange rate is the wrong weapon with which to attack current-account imbalances.

estimate Verb. *estimate* ['estɪmeɪt] *something* ist ‚eine Aussage machen, die auf Schätzungen beruht'.
the difficulty in estimating growth in real GDP
Estimating money demand may be well-nigh impossible. ... nahezu unmöglich.

Das Objekt kann auch aus *that*-Sätzen oder *wh*-Sätzen bestehen.
They can estimate how much people actually pay.
One recent study estimated that nearly 8% of Russia's current industrial output is value-subtracting.

Die Passivformen können durch *at* plus Zahl ergänzt werden.
Average growth in 1994 is estimated at 2.8%. ... wird auf ... geschätzt.

Das Partizip der Vergangenheit wird wie ein Adjektiv verwendet (‚geschätzt').
an estimated 18% last year
the estimated 80m
the estimated value of its assets

estimate Substantiv. *an estimate* ['estɪmət] ist eine Schätzung. Die geschätzte Sache usw. wird mit *of* eingeführt.
One estimate put income at $2,600.
based on the ICP estimates
estimates of the costs of production
America's estimate of the price of life
based on official Soviet estimates beruhend auf ...

expect. *expect something* ist ‚etwas erwarten'.
Gill & Duffus expect a world cocoa deficit of 110,000 tonnes this season.

Die entsprechende Passivkonstruktion ist möglich:
Real interest rates are roughly equal to nominal rates minus the inflation expected by the market.

expect kann mit einem *that*-Satz konstruiert werden. In dem Satz, der mit *that* angeschlossen wird, steht *will* oder ein anderes Hilfsverb, wie *can*.
That is one reason to expect that its rapid growth can continue.
Many economists expect that figures for total GDP, due on April 28th, will show annualised growth of almost 4%.

‚Erwarten, dass etwas geschieht' kann mit Substantiven plus *to*-Infinitiv formuliert werden.

They now expect inflation to rise to 3.4% next year.
Investors expect profits to rise.

Die insgesamt häufigste Konstruktion im Passiv ist *something/someone is expected* plus *to*-Infinitiv. Die Erwartenden werden dabei nicht genannt.
Growth is expected to slow in both economies next year.
Russian exports are expected to fall.
China is expected to import some 9m tonnes.

expectation Substantiv. *expectations* (üblicherweise als Plural) sind die Erwartungen.
Das, worauf sich die Erwartungen beziehen, kann über Adjektive oder Substantive vor dem *expectations* formuliert werden:
... *signalling lower inflationary expectations.* in Bezug auf niedrigere Inflation
business expectations Geschäftserwartungen
market expectations Markterwartungen

Die Konstruktion mit *'s* nennt die Erwartenden:
the market's inflationary expectations

Längere Konstruktionen vor *expectations* werden vermieden, stattdessen steht *expectations of*. Was nach dem *of* steht, entspricht dem Objekt zu *expect,* es sind ‚Erwartungen von'.
expectations of much higher company earnings

Mit *about* wird angeschlossen, wenn Erwartungen hinsichtlich einer Sache oder Person ausgedrückt werden sollen.
expectations about inflation
investors' expectations about the relative tightness of monetary policy in America and Japan

Nach *expectations* kann ein *that*-Satz stehen.
First, a company's share price may soar because investors have realistic expectations that the firm concerned will earn fat profits in future.

fear Verb, Substantiv. Siehe *fear* in GEFAHREN, PROBLEME, SCHWIERIGKEITEN.

forecast, forecast, forecast Verb. Für die Voraussage wirtschaftlicher und finanzieller Entwicklungen ist *forecast* eine zentrale Wortform.

Subjekte zu *forecast* sind in der Regel Personen (vor allem Experten und Auguren) und Institutionen.

Eine der Konstruktionen ist *forecast something*.
The OECD forecasts growth for industrial economies of 3%.

Nach *forecast* kann ein *that*-Satz stehen. Die Voraussagenden werden genannt, die Voraussage wird mit *that* eingeführt. Im *that*-Satz steht *will*, wenn *forecast* im Präsens steht.
The OECD forecasts that inflation will pick up slightly. ... dass die Inflation leicht zunimmt.

Die häufigste Konstruktion ist *someone/something is forecast* plus *to*-Infinitiv. In dieser Konstruktion wird die Person oder Institution, die die Voraussage macht, nicht genannt.
Italy's economy is forecast to grow by 2.2% this year.
Russian sales are forecast to rise by 18% to 800,000 ounces.
This year consumption is forecast to recover to 100,000 tonnes.

Das Partizip der Vergangenheit wird als Adjektiv verwendet.
a forecast deficit of 7.6% this year ein vorausgesagtes Defizit ...

forecast Substantiv. *forecasts* (meist in der Pluralform) sind Vorhersagen, Voraussagen. Der Bereich, auf den sich die Voraussage bezieht, kann als Adjektiv oder Substantiv vor dem *forecast* stehen.
economic forecasts
currency forecasts
growth forecasts
inflation forecast

Vorgestellte Substantive können auch den Voraussagenden bezeichnen oder eine sonstige Qualität der Voraussage.
OECD forecasts
consensus forecasts

Die Art der Voraussage kann dem *forecast* vorgestellt sein:
11% GDP growth forecast

Die Konstruktion *x's forecast* gibt entweder den Zeitpunkt der Voraussage an oder die Voraussagenden.
the previous month's forecast
the panel's forecasts

Der Anschluss mit *for* gibt die zeitliche Geltungsdauer an oder verweist auf den Geltungsbereich.

the forecast for January
the forecast for three/six months
the forecast for the rouble

Das Objekt der Voraussage wird mit *of* angeschlossen.

an official forecast of $8 billion
its forecast of inflation
forecasts of GDP growth

Voraussagen, die auf etwas beruhen, sind *based on something*.

forecasts based on the latest poll

Gelegentlich werden Voraussagen nach oben korrigiert (*raised*), nach unten korrigiert (*trimmed*) oder allgemein revidiert (*revised*).
The 1995 inflation forecast has also been raised sharply for Spain.
It trimmed its 1995 forecast for Japan to 2.2%.
They have revised their growth forecasts for 1994 up by 0.2 percentage points.

forecasts können auf etwas hinweisen (*indicate*), etwas annehmen (*assume*), etwas nahelegen (*suggest*).

forecaster. *forecasters* sind Personen, die Voraussagen erstellen.

future. Siehe *future* in ZEIT, dort in „2.3 Zukunft".

opinion. *an opinion* ist ‚eine Meinung'
opinions of American economists

Das Wort tritt häufig mit *public* auf, *public opinion* ‚öffentliche Meinung'.
division of opinion die unterschiedlichen Ansichten

likely. *likely* ist ein Adjektiv mit der Bedeutung ‚wahrscheinlich'.
Nastier outcomes are more likely.
faced with likely bankruptcy

Häufiger sind die Konstruktionen *it is/seems likely that* bzw. *someone/something is likely* plus *to*-Infinitv (siehe aber *probably* in diesem Abschnitt).

And it is likely that poor countries have bigger 'informal' economies than do rich ones.
Germany is likely to face criticism over its high interest rates.
It seems likely to be a highly inefficient deal.
Die Negation dazu ist *unlikely.*
The central bank is unlikely to cut interest rates.

more likely/most likely kann als Satzadverb im Sinne von ‚wahrscheinlicher noch/ am wahrscheinlichsten ist, dass' verwendet werden.

outlook. *the outlook* steht für die ‚Aussichten'.
The economic outlook for New Zealand is good.
The reason may be that investors remain worried about the longer-term outlook for American inflation.
The OECD provides some answers in its latest Employment Outlook.
The IMF has published its World Economic Outlook, with its new forecasts for the world economy.
Diese Zusammenstellungen des Internationalen Währungsfonds werden auch als *Economic Outlook* oder nur als *Outlook* bezeichnet.

possible. Das Adjektiv *possible* ist ‚möglich'.
the possible paths of development
Such collapse in trade is possible.

Das Adjektiv kann mit *to* plus Infinitiv oder mit einem *that*-Satz erweitert werden.
It may indeed be possible to avoid an inflationary surge.
It is possible that it may have a greater influence.

'so x wie möglich' ist *as x as possible.*
The question is how to keep tax rates as low as possible.

Das Adverb ist *possibly.*
possibly harmful
a possibly short-lived opportunity
Possibly, trade sanctions in these circumstances might change labour standards here and there. Möglicherweise ...

Das Substantiv ist *possibility.*
There is no possibility of changing the exchange rate.

One possibility is that ...
the possibility that ...

predict Verb. *predict* ‚voraussagen' ist seltener als *forecast.*
They also predict a plunge in the value of the Russian rouble.
He predicts that the euro and the dollar could eventually end up with a 40 per cent share each of international financial transactions.
At the other extreme, Japan is predicted to be the OECD's fastest grower in 1991.
Demand for palladium is predicted to climb by 12% to 4.7m ounces.

prediction Substantiv. *prediction* ‚Voraussage' ist seltener als *forecast.*
Every month The Economist polls a group of forecasters and calculates the average of their predictions for each of 15 countries.
their 1994 growth predictions

probably. Das Adverb *probably* ist ‚wahrscheinlich'. Das entsprechende Adjektiv ist *probable,* dieses ist jedoch selten; in der Regel wird das Adjektiv *likely* verwendet.
probably accidental wahrscheinlich zufällig
They were probably right.
The answer is probably no.
Das Substantiv ist *probability.*
a 75% probability of making the right choice

reckon Verb. *reckon* ist ‚(ein)schätzen, mit etwas rechnen'. Die häufigste Konstruktion ist *reckon* mit einem *that*-Satz ‚damit rechnen, dass'. Das *that* kann auch weggelassen werden. Im Passiv ist eine Ergänzung mit *to* plus Infinitiv möglich.
The McKinsey report reckons that the gap between savings and investment (i.e., the need for foreign capital) is likely to widen.
Mr Winston reckons the economists made two mistakes.
America's Internal Revenue Service is reckoned to have been $127 billion short (2% of GDP) in 1992.

Gelegentlich werden Substantiv und Verb umgestellt.
This is no surprise, the study reckons.
Another risk, reckons Mr Kaufman, is that ...

seem. Das Verb *seem* ‚scheinen' wird mit einem Adjektiv (nicht mit einem Adverb) oder einer Substantivkonstruktion ergänzt.
This may seem a dull question.
To many Britons this may seem perverse.
Vor Substantivkonstruktionen kann *like* stehen.
This may seem like a mighty complicated affair.
seem kann mit einem *that*-Satz oder mit einem *to*-Infinitv erweitert werden.
It seems that they were wrong.
The gold standard seemed to work well.
This seems to be the case.
Currency forecasters seem to be in unusual agreement ...
John Major seemed to have got his numbers wrong.

‚Wie es scheint' ist *as it seems*. *it seems* kann auch zwischen Kommas verwendet werden.
Wise investors, it seems, should watch exchange rates closely.

Um das ‚scheinen' noch vorsichtiger zu formulieren, geht *seem* zusätzlich mit *may* oder *would*: *It may/would seem that* ... Zu diesem Zweck können auch entsprechende Adjektive verwendet werden: *It seems probable/likely/plausible/reasonable/ sensible that ...*

seer Substantiv. *seers* ['si:əz] sind Voraussagende, Auguren (in Börsenberichten).
The currency seers expect the dollar to rise against the D-mark over the next year.

suppose. *suppose* wird zum Teil (mit *that*-Satz, bei dem das *that* meist weggelassen werden kann) verwendet, um ‚angenommen, dass' zu formulieren.
Suppose some firms are importing a chemical with a purity that the domestic chemical makers cannot match.
Suppose that there is a 75% chance that ...
it is supposed ‚wie angenommen wird' kann zwischen Kommas verwendet werden.
Germany, it is supposed, can easily afford to pay the bill.

Die Passivkonstruktion *something/someone is supposed to* plus Infinitiv bedeutet, dass etwas oder jemand so sein sollte, dass von einer Sache oder von jemandem erwartet oder doch wohl angenommen werden kann.
But economists are supposed to be above anecdote.

Foreign aid is supposed to fill that gap.
German unification was supposed to create another economic miracle.
Das Partizip der Vergangenheit kann als Adjektiv verwendet werden.
So much for the market's supposed foresight.

Dazu das Adverb *supposedly*.
At first, the Bank of Japan was supposedly going to cut its discount rate ... Zunächst war angenommen worden, dass ...

tend. Das Verb *tend* wird mit *to* und Infinitiv ergänzt. Es kann bedeuten, dass jemand zu etwas neigt.
Economists tend to see [this] as a necessary evil.

Ansonsten ist die Bedeutung ‚eine beobachtbare Tendenz haben' oder ‚aufgrund der Natur der Sache/möglicherweise zu einer bestimmten Entwicklung führen'.
Sterling tended to decline throughout the rest of the month.
Rates have tended to edge up recently.
Under free trade, wages will tend to converge in different countries.

Das Substantiv *tendency* ‚Neigung, Tendenz, Entwicklung' wird mit *toward* ‚zu' ergänzt. Komplexere Ergänzungen sind sind *a tendency for something/someone to do something* und *a tendency of something/someone to do something*.
History shows little tendency for real wages to revert to a 'normal' level, and real wage losses are never entirely regained. ... zeigt in Bezug auf Reallöhne nur eine geringe Tendenz...
the tendency of governments to tell lies die Neigung von Regierungen, Lügen zu erzählen

trend. *a trend (towards something)* kann ein Trend zu etwas sein. Diese Verwendung von *trend* ist selten, *trend* bezeichnet fast immer einen Verlauf, eine Entwicklung.
upward trend Aufwärtsbewegung, Konjunkturanstieg
downward trend
upward trend of prices
productivity trend Produktivitätsentwicklung
trend analysis Konjunkturanalyse

trends in something (seltener *of something*) sind die Verläufe, Entwicklungen in einem bestimmten Bereich.

the trend in labour productivity
the trend of labour productivity
future trends in industrial production
trends in poverty in Latin America

Entwicklungen über längere Zeit sind *trends over x.*
the downward trend over the past five years

trend wird nicht mit einem *that*-Satz ergänzt, wie es die deutsche Formulierung, die Entwicklung, dass; der Trend, dass' nahelegt.

view. *a view* ist eine Ansicht, Einschätzung, ein Standpunkt.
But this traditional view is coming under attack.
a person's views on something ist eine persönliche Meinung.
His views on the tariff are an oft-cited example of this [i.e., changing opinions].

a person's view (meist Singular) *of something* ist eine Einstellung, die einer Sicht oder Untersuchung zugrundeliegt.
cynical types with a low view of human nature

In jeder Bedeutung kann *view/views* mit einem *that*-Satz ergänzt werden.
arguments to refute the view that the GATT has outlived its usefulness

Weitere Phrasen:
from this point of view von diesem Standpunkt aus
in our view nach unserer Sicht
on this view so gesehen
in view of aus Sicht von, eingedenk

dissenting/competing/conflicting/radical/traditional views
to hold/support, take, refute a view

FINANCE, FINANCIAL

finance Verb. *finance* ['faɪnænts] ist ‚Geld für etwas zur Verfügung stellen; finanzieren'. Es wird mit direktem Objekt konstruiert.
America could not expect to finance such a deficit indefinitely.
the effort to finance the deficit

Die Finanzierenden (auch die Quelle) können mit *by* benannt werden. Die Quelle wird auch mit *from* oder *out of* genannt.
Most of this investment will be financed by domestic savings.
[It] was financed by the Bank.
financed from domestic savings
Dazu *financeable* ‚finanzierbar'.
a readily financeable current-account deficit.

finance Substantiv. Der Plural *(someone's) finances* kann mit ‚(jemandes) Finanzen' übersetzt werden.
Polish and Hungarian finances are not so healthy.
[This] would make the government's finances look even shakier. ... noch schwächer aussehen lassen
It is not only their own finances that will be at risk.

finance (nur im Singular und ohne den Artikel *a*) ist das Geld, das man für eine Unternehmung oder einen Kauf braucht.
The American subsidiaries of Japanese firms usually choose to raise finance in the American domestic market. ... entscheiden sich gewöhnlich dafür, das Kapital auf dem amerikanischen Binnenmarkt zu beschaffen.

Ansonsten ist *finance* (im Singular und ohne den Artikel *a*) der Umgang mit Geldangelegenheiten, besonders auf höheren Ebenen der Regierung und Verwaltung und bei größeren Unternehmen.
finance director
Ministry of Finance
finance ministry
finance minister
international finance
public finance

financial. *financial* [faɪ'nænʃəl] wird verwendet, um ‚finanziell, fiskalisch, geldlich' auszudrücken bzw. ‚Finanz-, Geld-, Geschäft-'.
financial accounts Finanzkonten
financial assets finanzielle Vermögenswerte
financial crash, financial crisis
financial deregulation
financial difficulties, financial disaster, financial fiasco

financial economics Finanzökonomie
financial health
financial help
financial innovation
financial instruments
financial markets Finanzmärkte
financial planning
financial reform
financial stability
financial system

Das Adverb hierzu ist *financially*.
financially dependent

GEFAHREN, PROBLEME, SCHWIERIGKEITEN

alarm. Wenn Gefahr droht, mag es nötig sein *to set the alarm bells ringing*. Substantiv und Verb *alarm* werden mit *at* oder *about* konstruiert. Aussichten, Untersuchungen, Zustände können *alarming* sein.
the dollar's alarming weakness
The study is also alarming.

Meistens ist jedoch von falschem Alarm die Rede.
There was a false alarm a year ago.
a false alarm about future inflation

damage Substantiv. *damage* ‚Schaden, Wertminderung, Beeinträchtigung' hat keine Pluralform, man kann daher nicht von *a damage* sprechen.
Under pessimistic assumptions, damage could be nearly 20% of world GDP ... könnte der Schaden ...

‚Schäden an der Umwelt' wird mit *environmental damage* wiedergegeben.

damage wird mit *to* erweitert, auch mit *(the damage) done to*.
valuing damage to the environment

Falls die Pluralform *damages* dennoch erscheint, so gehört sie zur Rechtssprache: ‚durch Urteil festgesetzte Zahlung an andere, Schadensersatz'.
awarding courtroom damages

damage Verb. *damage* ist ‚schädigen, beschädigen, Schaden zufügen'. Nach *damage* werden keine Objekte verwendet, die Personen bezeichnen, siehe *harm* in diesem Abschnitt.
America's inflationary policies damaged the dollar.
... anything that damages the economy.

danger. Eine bestimmte Situation kann als *danger* ‚Gefahr' (auch im Plural) eingeschätzt werden. Die Lage ist dann *dangerous (for somebody/something)* oder *dangerously* plus Adjektiv. *danger* wird mit *of* spezifiziert. *be in danger of doing something* ist ‚es besteht die Gefahr, dass jemand etwas tut'.
this danger
Rigid monetary rules are dangerous.
The lira is dangerously close to its permitted floor. ... gefährlich nah am unteren Interventionspunkt.
the possible danger of a devaluation
the dangers of smoking

difficult. Situationen und Handlungen können *difficult* sein.
difficult concessions
difficult economic choices schwierige wirtschaftliche Entscheidungen
He lucidly explains many difficult ideas.

difficult for someone to do something bedeutet: Es ist schwierig für jemanden, etwas zu tun.
This helps explain why it is often so difficult for groups of firms to agree a standard among themselves. Dies ist mit eine Erklärung, warum es für Firmen untereinander oft so schwierig ist ...

Die häufigste Konstruktion ist *(be) difficult* plus *to*-Infinitiv.
It is difficult to calculate real rates.
Fluctuations in profits are difficult to explain to irate investors ... Es ist schwierig ...
Markets may have found it difficult to match supply with demand.
A market, once lost, is difficult to recapture.

difficulty. Es gibt gelegentlich eine schwierige Situation oder Schwierigkeiten.
Mr Clinton's difficulties are not unique.
But there are difficulties.
But there is a difficulty.

Schwierigkeiten *lie somewhere* oder *are in something.*
The other difficulty lies in drawing a conclusion.
The biggest difficulty might be in persuading republics that ...

difficulty wird mit *in* oder *of* plus Verb-*ing* ergänzt.
the difficulty of transforming socialist economies
the difficulty in estimating growth in real GDP ...

the difficulty is that ... die Schwierigkeit besteht darin, dass ...

fear Verb. Die Konstruktionen für *fear* ‚befürchten' sind *fear something, fear that ...* Im *that*-Satz steht gewöhnlich *will* oder ein anderes Hilfsverb. ‚um etwas fürchten' ist *fear for.*
Many governments fear a high real exchange rate.
They fear that higher rates will strangle investment in the developed world.
[the Tories] fearing for their majorities ...

fear Substantiv. ‚Befürchtungen hinsichtlich' sind *fears about something.*
Are such fears about the impoverishment of unskilled workers in rich countries justified? ... solche Befürchtungen hinsichtlich der Verarmung ungelernter Arbeiter ...

‚Furcht vor' ist *fear of,* ‚aus Furcht vor' ist *for fear of.*
Both governments have been wary of greater international use of their currencies, for fear of losing control of their monetary policy.
The Bundesbank's fear of inflation ...
If you devalue today, you calm fears of a devaluation next week.

fear und *fears* können mit *that* ergänzt werden.
Stockmarkets stumbled this week because of fears that strong economic growth would prompt central banks in America and Britain to raise interest rates again to hold down inflation.

‚Befürchtungen vor etwas haben' kann auch mit *be fearful of* ausgedrückt werden.
fearful of terrorism
fearful of losing control

harm. Das Verb *harm* bedeutet ‚Schaden zufügen'. Nach *harm* können jedoch, anders als bei *damage*, Objekte stehen, mit denen Personen bezeichnet werden.
Such instability would harm the whole world economy.
Hostile takeovers may, in fact, harm shareholders.

Das Substantiv *harm* kann mit *to* ergänzt werden.
to minimise harm to the economy
Das Adjektiv ist *harmful*.
Can too little information be as harmful for an economy as too much?

hurt, hurt, hurt. *hurt* kann verwendet werden, um stärkere negative Auswirkungen auf jemanden oder etwas zu bezeichnen.
American consumers have been hurt by tumbling interest rates.
Sanctions hurt the countries imposing them. Die Sanktionen waren zum Schaden gerade derjenigen Länder, die sie eingerichtet haben.

Das Verb *injure* wird nur dann gebraucht, wenn von körperlichen Verletzungen (etwa im Zusammenhang mit Versicherungen oder gefährlichen Arbeitsplätzen) die Rede ist.

lose, loss. Siehe den Abschnitt *LOSE - LOSS*.

negative. Das Adjektiv *negative* wird verwendet, um (zahlenmäßig) negative Werte auszudrücken, jedoch auch im Sinne von ‚schlecht, schädlich'.
negative real interest rates
a negative discount rate
a negative inflation rate
a negative signal to consumers

problem. *a problem* bezeichnet in der Regel eine tatsächlich schwierige Situation – das Wort wird also nicht wie das deutsche „Problem" verwendet, das oft ‚Frage', ‚Gegenstand der Diskussion' bedeutet.
problems können durch Substantive und durch Adjektive näher definiert werden. Kombinationen mit Adjektiven sind: *economic, concrete, global, serious, common, big, environmental, fundamental, structural, financial, fiscal, complex, political problems*. Kombinationen mit Substantiven sind: *competitiveness problems, supply problems, measurement problems*.

problem for erläutert, wer sich mit einer Schwierigkeit auseinandersetzen muss.
This is a particularly serious problem for countries such as Zambia.

Die ‚Probleme von etwas': *problem/problems of.*
the problems of short-term management
the problems of financial adjustment
the measurement problems of price indices

Beachte, dass ‚das Problem, wie/wann/ob' ebenfalls als *problem of* konstruiert wird.
the problems of separating cause and effect
Russia also faces the problem of whether price liberalisation can be achieved in a heavily monopolised economy. ... das Problem, ob ...

Probleme mit etwas: *problems with.*
Japan's problems with high-definition television

Satzanfänge wie ‚Das Problem ist' gehen mit *the problem is* (*that/how* usw.).
The problem is that here Germany's interests are the exact opposite of France's.
The real problem is how can America cut its budget deficit.
One of the problems is definition.

Verben mit *problem* als Objekt: lösen: *solve*; angehen: *tackle, deal with, address*; erkennen: *recognise, diagnose*; haben: *have, be faced with*; untersuchen: *analyse*.

risk Verb. *risk something* bedeutet, dass man etwas tut und sich dabei einer Gefahr oder einem Nachteil aussetzt. Das Objekt kann auch mit einer *-ing-* Form eines Verbs angeschlossen werden.
Few citizens should risk cheating the taxman.
his willingness to risk a bit more inflation
The entrepreneur, risking everything in pursuit of a winning idea ...

risk Substantiv. Zur Beschreibung von Gefahr oder Risiko ist das Substantiv *risk* das am häufigsten gebrauchte. Es geht in verschiedene Konstruktionen ein.
There is one main risk in developing an oil field ... Es gibt ein wesentliches Risiko, wenn man ... /beim ...
The risk is that it may not last.
But the risk of a breakdown is real.
the risk of a recession
the incalculable risk that the consequences of climate change might be catastrophic. ... das Risiko/die Gefahr, dass ...

Wenn etwas *at risk* ist, dann steht es auf dem Spiel.

Kombinationen mit Verb plus *risk*:
Ein Risiko verringern: *reduce*; widerspiegeln: *reflect*; eingehen: *take* (und hierzu *risk-taking* als Substantiv), *run the risk of*; akzeptieren: *accept*; ignorieren: *ignore*. Einem Risiko entgegenwirken: *counter*. Ein Risiko entstehen lassen: *raise*.

risk kann auch durch vorangestellte Substantive und Adjektive näher definiert werden:
foreign exchange risk
currency risk
residual risk Restrisiko
economic risks
price risks

Im Kontext des Versicherungswesens ist *risk* auch der Versicherungsgegenstand.

risky, riskiness. Handlungen, Dinge, Zustände, die *risky* sind, bergen eine Gefahr, aufgrund inhärenter Unsicherheiten.
the unusual riskiness of environmental decisions
unduly risky for lenders
risky assets risikobehaftete Anlagen
a risky course eine riskante Politik

threat. Eine drohende Entwicklung oder Bedrohung (für jemanden/etwas) ist *a threat* [θret] *to someone/something*.
the threat to the world's climate

Die Bedrohung oder Drohung durch etwas ist *a threat of* bzw. *a threat that*.
the threat of imminent disaster
the threat of unilateral sanctions
... the threat that benefits will not be paid if the claimant does not search for work or accept job offers.

threaten. Das Verb *threaten* ['θretən] kann bedeuten ‚etwas enthält die Gefahr von ...'. Eine Ergänzung mit *to* plus Verb ist möglich, ebenfalls eine Ergänzung mit *with*.
A rapid decline in interest rates would threaten a repeat of the credit-fuelled consumer boom of 1987-88.

The weakness of the D-mark threatens to fuel inflation. ... droht die Inflation anzuheizen.

... which threatens the unemployed with poverty ... was für die Arbeitslosen die Gefahr der Armut bedeutet

Personen, Institutionen usw. können *threaten to do something,* also ‚(damit) drohen (dass)'.
The car makers of America have threatened to bring anti-dumping suits against car importers.

trouble. *troubles* (in der Pluralform) bezeichnet Schwierigkeiten in einem bestimmten Bereich: *fiscal troubles, political troubles, money troubles, economic troubles.* Die Singularform wird vor allem in Wendungen gebraucht, wie *be in trouble, get into trouble, run into trouble* (geraten), *the trouble is that ..., someone has trouble doing something, the trouble with ...*
a troubled firm ist eine Firma, die in finanzielle Schwierigkeiten geraten ist.

warn, warning. Das Verb *warn* ‚auf Gefahr aufmerksam machen' wird meist zusammen mit einem *that*-Satz verwendet.
The committee warns that policy is too lax.

Zwischen Kommas und mit einem vorangestellten Subjekt wie *he, it, they* steht es im Sinne von ‚so seine/ihre Warnung'.
This excess liquidity, it warns, has driven up prices. ... so die Warnung ...

warning ist die Warnung, in den Konstruktionen *give warning that* oder *give warning of.*
To many people these figures give warning of a worrying loss of competitiveness.
The IMF gives warning that America's spare capacity is likely to be fully absorbed during the course of the year.

Entwicklungen oder Beobachtungen, die als „Frühwarnsignale" interpretiert werden können, sind *early-warning indicators* oder *early-warning signals.*

worry Verb. *worry* ‚sich Sorgen machen, besorgt sein, größere Bedenken haben' tritt meist mit der Ergänzung *about* auf, auch mit einem folgenden *that*-Satz; es wird selten für sich alleine verwendet.
Consumers have had much to worry about in the past couple of years.
[They] did not need to worry about popular resentment.

Conventional economists worry that special treatment for the environment may lead to perverse results.
[They] said yes, they had worried.
If so, why worry?

Das Partizip *worrying* kann wie ein Adjektiv verwendet werden.
a worrying loss of competitiveness
a worrying 8.8%

worried kann mit *be* (oder ähnlichen Verben wie *seem, become*) und *about* konstruiert werden.
... investors remain worried about the longer-term outlook.

worry Substantiv. Das Substantiv hat Ergänzungen mit *about* bzw. einem *that*-Satz.
worries about inflation
One particular worry is that Japan could find itself with outright deflation.
... because of worries that figures for September would show a big increase

GEGENSATZ UND EINRÄUMUNG

Gegensätze sind in Wirtschaftsberichten häufig enthalten, z.B. *rise – fall, high – low, now – then*.
In diesem Abschnitt wird jedoch nur behandelt, wie man Gegensatz (und Einräumung) explizit ausdrückt.

admit. *admit* ist ‚zugeben, einräumen', meist mit einem folgenden *that*-Satz oder einem *wh*-Satz.
The World Bank admits that the extent to which Sub-Saharan Africa can copy Malaysia ... is limited.
Few manufacturers admit how much they rely on services. ... geben zu, wie stark sie Dienstleistungen in Anspruch nehmen.

‚Man muss zugeben' ist *it must be admitted (that)*.
admittedly ist ‚zugegeben ..., wie man zugeben muss'.
This is admittedly a simplification. Das ist, zugegeben, eine Vereinfachung.

Admittedly, the impact of house prices on GDP is probably two or three times as great as that of commercial-property prices.

albeit. albeit [ɔːlˈbiːɪt] wird in formelleren Texten im Sinne von ‚wenngleich, obwohl' verwendet. Es wird bevorzugt eingesetzt, um eine Art von Nachgedanken auszudrücken, meist folgt eine Struktur, die kein Verb hat.
... recession did follow, albeit with a longer lag than normal. ... wenngleich mit größerer Verzögerung als normal.
In America, consumer confidence, retail sales and housing starts are pointing to a recovery, albeit a slow one. ... deuten auf eine wirtschaftliche Erholung, wenngleich eine allmähliche.

although. although [ɔːlˈðəʊ] ist ‚obwohl, wenngleich'. Der Nebensatz mit *although* kann vor oder nach dem Hauptsatz stehen. Im Unterschied zu *though* stehen die Sätze mit *although* jedoch meist an der Spitze.
Although interest rates around the world have soared this year, borrowing on the international capital markets has continued to rise.
More than 90% of foreign direct investment (FDI) originates in OECD countries, although in 1993 outflows from these countries fell by 3% while inflows soared by 11%.

but. but ‚aber' ist eine Konjunktion, die zwei Hauptsätze miteinander verbindet. Das *but* steht vor dem zweiten Hauptsatz.
France is also a high-tax country, but it collects a relatively small share of its revenues through income taxes.

but kann einen einzelnen Satz einleiten. Dann kontrastiert die Aussage dieses Satzes mit der des vorangehenden Satzes.
But that does not mean that everything costs more.
Madrid rose 4.8% and Hong Kong 4.0%. But IBM's losses helped depress Wall Street.

Für den Fall, dass die beiden Sätze das gleiche Subjekt haben, kann dieses im *but*-Satz ausgelassen werden.
Britain's retail sales fell 0.7% in December, but were 1.2% up on the year.
Germany's GNP fell by 0.5% in the third quarter, but was 1.9% higher than a year earlier.

Weitergehende Auslassungen sind ebenfalls möglich.
America's industrial production was unchanged in September, but still 6.6% higher than a year earlier.

but kann innerhalb einer Reihe von Adjektiven oder Adverbien einen Gegensatz bezeichnen.
New (but delayed) figures for Holland ...
but kann durch andere Konjunktionen erweitert werden, wie *but if* ‚aber wenn', *but while* ‚aber während', *but because* ‚aber weil, aber da'.
But because the market's inflationary expectations cannot be measured directly ...
But while India is becoming a slightly safer country for investors, the risks involved in China are increasing.

Weitere Ausführungen zu *but* siehe Abschnitt *BUT.*

concede. *concede* (meist mit *that*-Satz) ist ‚einräumen'.
to concede a point ein Gegenargument anerkennen
Mr Frankel concedes that Japan's direct investment in the Asian region has risen from $2 billion in 1985 to a hefty $8.2 billion in 1988.

contrary. Die Phrase *on the contrary* bedeutet ‚im Gegenteil, im Gegensatz'.
... on the contrary, such changes were nothing but a nuisance.

evidence to the contrary ist Beweismaterial dafür, dass etwas ganz anderes der Fall ist.

Mit *contrary to* wird ‚im Gegensatz zu' (meist in Bezug auf Ansichten) formuliert.
contrary to popular belief
contrary to most assumptions
contrary to the textbook view im Gegensatz zu den Handbüchern

contrast Substantiv. Mit *by contrast* oder *in contrast* wird ein Gegensatz ausdrücklich genannt.
The average American today lives for 76 years. By contrast, because of disease and malnutrition, the average life expectancy at birth in the Sudan is a mere 51 years.
Britain's yield curve, by contrast, is still slightly inverted.
In Russia, by contrast, where the transition process started later and has been slower, job losses have been relatively modest.
In contrast Chrysler made a mere 12% of its sales abroad ...

Caracas fell by 6.0%, Athens by 3.2% and Istanbul by 2.4%. In contrast, there were bullish markets in Taipei, up by 10.3%, ...

despite. Die Präposition *despite* ist ‚trotz'.
New York reached an all-time high despite continued economic gloom.
Despite a massive drop in output in Russia, its official unemployment rate remains low.

despite wird auch als Konjunktion verwendet. Das Verb (im Beispielsatz *lose*) steht dann in einer *-ing*-Form. Die Bedeutung ist ‚obwohl, wenngleich'.
Asian share prices have risen most, more than doubling during the period – despite losing some ground in 1994.

distinction. Ein Gegensatz oder Unterschied zu ist *a distinction (between)*.
The distinction between capital and current spending is often unclear.

even. *even so* ist ‚selbst dann, selbst wenn dies der Fall ist/sein sollte', ‚dennoch'. Mit diesem *even so* wird etwas eingeführt, das irgendwie überraschend oder unerwartet ist.
The ratio of stocks to consumption is set to fall to 53%, the lowest for five years. Even so, world stocks could be a hefty 1.3m tonnes at the end of the season.

even though drückt aus, dass man zwar einen Gegensatz konstatiert (im Beispielsatz: *inflation remains low*), dass dieser Gegensatz aber die Gültigkeit der restlichen Aussage (im Beispielsatz: *policy-makers have started to increase interest rates*) nicht tangiert.
First in America and now in Britain policy-makers have started to increase interest rates even though inflation remains low. ... trotz der Tatsache, dass die Inflation niedrig bleibt.

even if/when entspricht ‚selbst, wenn'.
Even if trade was to blame for the slump in real wages of low-skilled workers, protectionism would therefore not be the answer.
Average tax rates may be low even when marginal rates are high.

however. *however* ‚jedoch' drückt einen Gegensatz aus, und zwar so, dass dieser oft als etwas überraschend, nicht ganz so normal empfunden wird. *however* steht im

Satz an verschiedenen Positionen. Im Satzinneren steht es meist zwischen Kommas, am Satzanfang als *However, ...* und am Satzende als *..., however.*
Für den Satzanfang ist die Übersetzung ‚jedoch, dennoch'.
However, Britain is the only G7 economy in which public spending has fallen as a percentage of GDP since 1980.
However, many emerging equity markets have performed poorly this year.

Das *however* am Satzende ist ‚jedoch, allerdings'.
Methods of borrowing varied considerably, however.

Öfters steht *however* nach der ersten Phrase des Satzes, also z.B. nach dem ersten Adverbiale oder nach dem Subjekt: ‚jedoch, allerdings, aber'. Die Phrase erhält dadurch eine besondere Betonung.
The dollar-yen rate, however, is expected to remain broadly unchanged.
Cigarettes, however, are a third cheaper in Tokyo than in New York.

however steht auch unmittelbar nach dem Imperativ.
Note, however, the huge range of the forecasts for the rouble. Man beachte jedoch ...

Ansonsten kann *however* die üblichen Positionen von Adverbien einnehmen (nach einer einfachen Form von *be,* nach dem ersten Hilfsverb).
Developing countries have, however, been keener than industrialised ones to use the yen as a reserve currency.

however (ohne Kommas) vor Adjektiven, wie z.B. *however difficult* ist ‚wie ... auch, wie immer ... '.

in spite of. *in spite of* ist eine Mehrwortpräposition und bedeutet ‚trotz'.
Britain's net external balance has improved of late, in spite of current-account deficits.

nevertheless. *nevertheless* ‚nichtsdestoweniger, dennoch' steht zu Anfang des Satzes.
Nevertheless, the WTO could try to bring trade rules and competition rules together sooner rather than later.

nonetheless. Mit dem Adverb *nonetheless* wird ein Einwand oder Gegensatz entkräftet, ‚nichtsdestoweniger'. Im Unterschied zu *nevertheless* steht es auch im Satzinneren (in der Position für Adverbien).

The experiment must nonetheless be deemed a great success.
Nonetheless, Exxon is second to Nestle in the chart ...

opposite. Das Substantiv *opposite* ['ɒpəzɪt] ist ‚Gegenteil'.
Exactly the opposite has happened.
In Germany, the problem is the opposite.
Germany's interests are the opposite of France's.

Das Adjektiv *opposite* beschreibt etwas, das ganz anders ist.
the opposite direction
the opposite effect

still. Mit *still* (am Satzanfang und mit Komma) wird ein Einwand eingeleitet, der nicht besonders wichtig erscheint, also ‚aber dennoch, aber trotzdem, aber – '.
Still, these problems are not bad enough to invalidate the study.

Auch die Bedeutung ‚dennoch, immerhin' kann in Frage kommen.
Still, that would require a big change in thinking for today's politicians.

Weitere Bedeutungen von *still* siehe *still* in VERGLEICH, ÄHNLICHKEIT, UNTERSCHIED und in ZEIT, dort in „2.4 Gleichzeitigkeit".

though. *though* ist ‚obwohl, wenngleich'. Der Nebensatz mit *though* kann vor oder nach dem Hauptsatz stehen, die Stellung nach dem Hauptsatz ist bevorzugt (im Unterschied zu *although*).
Europeans, too, prefer Asia, though they have been keener than Americans and Japanese to invest in Eastern Europe and Southern Africa ...
Though few investors would believe it, stockmarket indices rarely end a year worth less, in nominal terms, than they began it.

Eine Konstruktion wie *Though it may be hard ...* kann, zur Betonung von *hard*, umgestellt werden zu *Hard though it may be ...* ‚Zwar mag es hart sein ....'

Zu *even though* siehe *even* in diesem Abschnitt.

though kann als Adverb (‚aber, jedoch, zwar') nach einer Phrase stehen und bezieht sich dann auf diese. Diese Verwendung ist für *although* nicht anzutreffen.
In both countries, though, output was up on the year. In beiden Ländern aber ...
In developing countries, though, the dollar has held its own.
Imports, though, continued to increase. Die Importe aber/jedoch ...

whereas. Die Konjunktion *whereas* leitet eine Art Kommentar ein, der ergänzende, aber gegensätzliche Information bringt: ‚während dagegen, wohingegen'.
This explains why the dollar has fallen by only 8% in trade-weighted terms over the past 12 months, whereas it has lost 10-18% against the yen and the main European currencies.
Changes in total fuel consumption are determined primarily by economic growth rates, whereas the mix of fuels used depends upon other factors.
Almost all Japanese equity flows went to other Asian countries, whereas Europeans split most of their equity investment almost equally between Asia and Latin America.

while. In der Gemeinsprache bedeutet *while* als Konjunktion auch ‚währenddessen'. Diese Bedeutung ist in Wirtschaftstexten nicht ausgeschlossen.
In fast allen Fällen werden aber Aussagen verbunden, die zueinander in einem Gegensatz stehen. Die Bedeutung von *while* ist daher ‚während dagegen, während im Gegensatz'. *while* kann mit *but* zu *but while* kombiniert werden.
Its output had increased by 25% in the four years to 1987, while Japan's had risen by a mere 14%.
Growth is expected to slow in both economies next year, while continental Europe and Japan are forecast to expand more briskly.
But while India is becoming a slightly safer country for investors, the risks involved in China are increasing.
Thailand's deficit remained at $8.4 billion in the 12 months to August, while over the same period Mexico's deficit edged up to $16.9 billion.
Siehe auch *when* in ZEIT, dort in „2.4 Gleichzeitigkeit".

yet. *yet* als Konjunktion ist ‚dennoch'. Nach diesem *yet* kann ein Komma stehen. Zu *yet* im Sinne von ‚noch, derzeit' siehe *yet* in ZEIT, dort in „2.4 Gleichzeitigkeit".
Yet the economic logic behind this notion is surprisingly weak.
Yet in both countries inflation remains subdued.
Yet the main message of a new report from McKinsey, a consultancy firm, is: 'don't panic'.
And yet the evidence that sanctions work is slight.

GEWINNE, EINKÜNFTE

earn. Die Bedeutung von *earn* hängt von den jeweils verwendeten Subjekten bzw. Objekten ab. Personen, Institutionen, Firmen ‚verdienen'.
Low-income Europeans earn 44% more per hour than low-income Americans.
Consultants earn fat fees.
[This] allows firms to earn big profits.
If all the oil, natural gas, gold, iron and other metals that Russia produces this year were exported ..., Russia would earn around about $110 billion.

earn wird verwendet, wenn Papiere, Anlagen usw. Rendite ‚bringen'.
... money-market mutual funds, which are not government-insured and earn higher rates of interest than traditional deposits. ... und höhere Zinsen bringen als die üblichen Einlagen.

Aus Sicht der Finanzbehörden ist *earn* ‚Steuereinnahmen erzielen'.
The Treasury will earn a meagre $3.4 billion extra each year.

earned income ist das Arbeits- bzw. Erwerbseinkommen, *earned income tax* ist die Einkommensteuer auf Löhne und Gehälter oder auf Einkommen aus selbständiger Tätigkeit.

earnings. earnings (ein Pluralwort) bezeichnet in den meisten Fällen das Gesamt an Geld, das einem Angestellten/Arbeiter in einem festen Abstand für die Arbeit gezahlt wird.
the loss in workers' earnings

earnings ist allerdings ähnlich mehrdeutig wie das Verb *earn* und kann allgemein ‚Verdienst, Einkünfte und Gewinne' bedeuten.
export earnings
foreign-currency earnings
price/earnings ratio Kurs-Gewinn-Verhältnis

fee. Mit *fee* (Plural *fees*) wird ‚Gebühr' bezeichnet.
payments of royalties and licence fees

Außerdem ist *fee* das Honorar, das für Leistungen bestimmter Berufsgruppen (z.B. Ärzte, Rechtsanwälte, Architekten, Gutachter) zu zahlen ist.
Consultants earn fat fees.

gain Verb. *gain* wird im Sinne von ‚einen finanziellen (oder sonstigen) Vorteil haben' ohne Objekt verwendet. In dieser Bedeutung kann es auch mit *from* konstruiert werden.
Consumers stand to gain. Die Verbraucher werden wahrscheinlich davon profitieren.
Since EFTA countries were small, the EC gained little from bringing them into the single market.

Mit Objekt kann *gain* ‚erreichen, erzielen' bedeuten.
They can gain a bigger share of high-definition television sales.

In Börsenberichten ist *gain* ‚sich erhöhen, gewinnen', besonders in Bezug auf den Kurs einer Währung.
In trade-weighted terms the dollar gained 2.8% during the week.

to gain control of something ist ‚etwas beherrschen, etwas in den Griff bekommen'.

gain Substantiv. *gain* kann ‚Vorteil, Nutzen' bedeuten.
The most important gain, however, could be better access to advanced technologies.

In den meisten Fällen ist die Bedeutung ‚(finanzieller) Zuwachs'. Eventuelle Zahlen werden mit *of* eingeführt. ‚Zuwächse aus einem Bereich' sind *gains from,* ‚Zuwächse in einem bestimmten Bereich' *gains in.*
In Mexico City, however, growing domestic optimism resulted in gains of 5.9%.
yield plus capital gains Rendite plus Kursgewinne
Milan was the star, with a gain of 8.2%.
the gains from working
the gains in efficiency

income. *income* ist Geld, das man regelmäßig erhält, etwa als Gehalt, Lohn, Honorar, auch als Kapitaleinkünfte, Miete usw. Etwaige Zahlen beziehen sich auf die Höhe pro Jahr. Der Plural *incomes* kann verwendet werden, wenn von verschiedenen Arten von Einkommen die Rede ist oder von den Einkommen mehrerer Personen, Institutionen.
an income of roughly $5,000
the income of savers
the income from working
people with high incomes
people underreporting their incomes to the taxman

incomes above $135,000
urban and rural incomes

earned income Arbeits-, Erwerbseinkommen
extra income Nebeneinkommen
disposable income frei verfügbares Einkommen
gross income Bruttoeinkommen
high income
low income
medium income
national income Volkseinkommen
net income Nettoeinkommen
real income Realeinkommen
unearned income Einkünfte aus Kapitalvermögen

Die meisten dieser Fügungen können insgesamt als Adjektiv verwendet werden, dann werden sie mit Bindestrich geschrieben, z.B. *high-income earners, national-income accounting, low-income Germans.*

income-per-head ‚Pro-Kopf-Einkommen' (auch: *per capita income*)
income tax Einkommensteuer
income tax rate
income tax cut
earned income tax Einkommensteuer auf Löhne und Gehälter oder auf Einkommen aus selbständiger Tätigkeit

pay Substantiv. *pay* – nur im Singular und ohne den unbestimmten Artikel *a* – ist Geld, das man für Arbeit erhält (siehe auch *salary, wage* in diesem Abschnitt), aber auch anderes erhaltenes Geld.
annual pay settlements jährliche Lohn- und Gehaltsvereinbarungen
Self-employment means long hours and little pay.
unemployment pay
a public-sector strike over pay
But pay is also low in communications and computing.
sick pay Krankengeld

payment. *payment* bezeichnet sowohl das Zahlen selbst als auch die gezahlte Summe. Es ist das Wort, mit dem die Zahlungsbedingungen (*payment terms*) formuliert werden:

payment on delivery Lieferung gegen bar (Nachnahme)
payment on request Zahlung auf Verlangen
payment by instalment Ratenzahlung

balance-of-payments Zahlungsbilanz
balance-of-payments deficit
balance of payments surplus

profit Substantiv. *profit* ist ‚Gewinn/Gewinne'. Das Substantiv kann mit dem unbestimmten Artikel *a* und auch als Pluralform (*profits*) verwendet werden, aber auch als Singularwort (ohne den unbestimmten Artikel *a*).
It can make a profit by renting the network.
Big fluctuations in profits are difficult to explain.
There is no need to argue how much profit a firm actually earned.

Wenn Adjektive vorangehen (wie *worldwide, greater, taxable, expected, soaring, future, current, extra, excessive, fat, hefty, monopolistic, predicted, higher, nominal*), wird die Pluralform *profits* verwendet.
Gewinne, die dadurch entstehen, dass man etwas tut, sind *profits by* plus Verb-*ing*.
Gewinne aus etwas sind *profits from*.
a profit by winning a particular licence
profits from the project

distributable profit ist ‚ausschüttbarer Gewinn'

Gewinn/Gewinne erzielen: *earn, make, produce, see*; maximieren: *maximise*; erwarten: *expect*; kalkulieren: *calculate*.

Das Adjektiv *profitable* ist ‚gewinnbringend, gewinnträchtig'. Das Substantiv dazu lautet *profitability*.
profitable investment opportunities.
a profitable new product
increases in expected profitability

return Substantiv. *a return* ist das Zurück zu einem vorherigen Zustand.
a gradual return to stronger real growth

in return ist ‚im Gegenzug'.
The idea is that dodgers [Steuerhinterzieher] *come out with their hands up and their wallets open; in return, the taxman promises not to prosecute.*

a tax return ist eine Steuererklärung.
Few Americans look forward to April 15th, the date by which they have to file their annual income-tax returns.

return bedeutet auch ‚Ertrag, Erträge (aufgrund von Investition, Anlage, Sparen)'. *return* ist Singularwort (ohne den unbestimmten Artikel *a*), kann aber auch mit Artikel und im Plural stehen.
the returns earned on the share
There is every reason to undertake investments that yield the highest returns.
Yet many, such as company pension funds, consistently fail to achieve even the average market return, largely because they over-invest in 'hot' stocks.
better returns from investment funds
the expected return on dollars (interest plus the expected change in the value of the currency)
the rate of return
share returns
the risk-return relationship
higher-return alternatives
equity returns
financial returns
stockmarket returns

revenue. Im Zusammenhang mit Steuer ist *revenue* ['revənju:] ‚Steuereinnahmen' des Staates (*tax revenue*). Ansonsten bezeichnet es Geld, das während einer bestimmten Zeit durch Verkäufe oder Leistungen eingeht. Die Singularform hat nicht den unbestimmten Artikel *a*.
Total railway revenues barely cover railway wage bills.
Deregulation tended to lower both costs and revenues.
timber revenue Einkünfte durch den Verkauf von Holz

salary. *a salary* ist das Gehalt, das Angestellte erhalten.
... because the salaries paid to top managers have soared.
wage and salary earners (in etwa) Lohn- und Gehaltsempfänger
at full salary bei vollem Gehalt

wage. *wage* im Singular wird teilweise unterschiedlich von *wages* (Plural) gebraucht.

wage kann allgemein das Geld bezeichnen, das für geleistete Arbeit bezahlt wird („Lohn'). *wage* ist auch das Geld, das auf der zeitlichen Basis von Stunden, Tagen, Wochen gezahlt wird.
wages ist der Lohn insbesondere für körperliche Arbeit oder das Gehalt für einfache Bürotätigkeiten (im Unterschied zum *salary*, s.o.), also ‚Löhne' bzw. ‚Gehälter'.

Wenn ein weiteres Substantiv folgt, steht *wage*: *wage accords, wage adjustment, wage behaviour, wage bill, wage cuts, wage differentials, wage explosion, wage flexibility, wage growth, wage inequalities, wage rises, wage reform, wage restraint, wage structure.*

Einige Zusammensetzungen, die als Adjektive fungieren, haben ebenfalls *wage*: *low-wage countries, a full-wage employee, real-wage growth, non-wage benefits, the minimum-wage idea.*

Nach einer Kombination von Substantiv plus Präposition steht meist *wages*.
inequality in wages Lohnungleichheit
distribution of wages
an explosion in wages
pressure on wages
disparities in wages

average wages Durchschnittslöhne
minimum wages Mindestlöhne
real wages Reallöhne

wages werden angepasst: *are adjusted*; werden gekürzt: *are cut*; verdoppeln sich: *double*; fallen: *fall*; werden erhöht/erhöhen sich: *are increased, are raised, rise.*

yield [ji:ld] Substantiv. *the yield* ist der Ertrag, den Investitionen oder Anlagen bringen, besonders festverzinsliche Wertpapiere.
the sharp increase in long-term bond yields
real bond yields
the yield on conventional government bonds
yields on long-term Treasury bonds
the yields on Germany's long-term government bonds
the yield curve
real yields

yield Verb. In Zusammenhang mit einem Objekt, das einen finanziellen Gewinn bezeichnet, bedeutet *yield* ‚einbringen, erbringen, abwerfen, als Ertrag haben'.

Since investment today yields benefits for future taxpayers, it may be reasonable to expect them to share some of the costs.
Besides generating environmental benefits, the energy tax would have yielded revenue.
investments that yield the highest returns
They will yield even bigger profits.
higher-yielding assets such as mutual funds

Mit Adverb oder Objekt ist *yield* ‚ergeben'.
30 years' negotiations have yielded little in the way of reform.
Putting the two together yields a true measure for the price of light.

yield to something bedeutet ein Nachgeben oder, wie im folgenden Satz, ein Zugänglich-Sein.
How far it will yield to theoretical analysis remains to be seen.

INFLATION

inflation wird nur im Singular gebraucht und ohne den unbestimmten Artikel *a*.
Inflation then accelerated a year later. Die Inflation beschleunigte sich dann im folgenden Jahr.
Inflation is still above 10%.

Eine Inflation während einer bestimmten Zeit kann als *inflationary era* oder *inflationary period* bezeichnet werden, im Plural dann *inflationary eras, periods*. Mit *inflation* (als erstem Teil) werden nur wenige Verbindungen gebildet. Siehe *inflationary* in diesem Eintrag.
inflation figures
inflation-fighting
inflation fears
inflation rate
inflation target   Inflationsvorgabe

In seltenen Fällen wird *inflation* auch als zweiter Teil in einer Verbindung gebraucht.
consumer-price inflation
double-digit inflation (rate)   zweistellige Inflationsrate

Modifikationen von *inflation* werden im allgemeinen über Adjektive formuliert: *accelerating, annual, average, domestic* (im Inland), *future, high, home-grown, increasing, little, low, zero.*

Verben mit *inflation* als Objekt: *be wary of* ‚sorgfältig beobachten, befürchten', *beat, bring down, bring under control, counter* ‚bekämpfen', *curb* ‚dämpfen, bremsen, zügeln', *combat* ‚bekämpfen', *cut, fight, fuel* ‚anheizen', *hold back, hold down, ignite* ‚entfachen', *increase, keep down, keep low, prevent, reduce.*

Verben mit *inflation* als Subjekt: *be harmful, become a problem, continue to ..., erode something* ‚den Wert von etwas mindern', *fall, increase, nudge 10%* ‚in die Nähe von 10% kommen', *pick up* ‚zunehmen', *remain ..., rise.*

Das Adjektiv *inflationary* dient zum Ausdruck sowohl von ‚inflationär' als auch von ‚Inflations-'.

a chaotic and inflationary economy
inflationary expectations Inflationserwartung
inflationary pressure Inflationsdruck
inflationary China

Es wird mit *non-* verneint.
non-inflationary growth

INTEREST

interest Verb. *Something interests someone* ist ‚etwas interessiert, beschäftigt jemanden'.
a problem that has increasingly interested economists

interest Substantiv. Die gemeinsprachliche Verwendung von *interest* kommt vor, besonders als *interest in something*; auch in Verbindungen, auch im Plural.
the new interest in growth theory
a keen interest in global economic stability starkes Interesse an ...
a legitimate interest in exerting pressure ein berechtigtes Interesse, Druck auszuüben
self-interest Eigeninteresse
producer interest das Interesse der Hersteller
political interests

of great interest von großem Interesse
public interest öffentliches Interesse

an interest kann eine Beteiligung oder ein Anteil sein. In der Bedeutung ‚Zins, Zins-' hat *interest* keine Pluralform und steht ohne den unbestimmten Artikel *a*.
interest (earned) on savings Zinsen auf Spareinlagen
bear interest Zinsen tragen
interest payments Zinszahlungen
interest rate Zins, Zinssatz
interest-rate cut Zinssenkung
interest-rate changes

interested Adjektiv. *be interested in* ist ‚Interesse haben an'.
Other countries will be interested in results too.

interesting. Das Adjektiv *interesting* bedeutet, dass etwas wert ist, weiter verfolgt zu werden, ‚interessant, diskutierenswert, reizvoll' usw.
an interesting question
an interesting case
There is nothing interesting to buy.

KOSTEN, INVESTITIONEN, SCHULDEN

borrow. *borrow* ist ‚borgen, Geld aufnehmen'. Das Verb kann für sich stehen, mit einem Objekt (das sich auf einen Betrag bezieht) verwendet werden und/oder mit einer *from*-Ergänzung (‚von jemandem'). Ein Zweck kann mit *for* konstruiert werden.
If businesses and consumers start borrowing again, it will fuel a recovery.
They will borrow a horrendous $10 trillion.
When Britain borrowed from the IMF in the 1970s ...
It is fine to borrow for investment.

Häufig ist die Verwendung des Substantivs *borrowing* ‚Schuldenaufnahme' (auch ‚Kreditbetrag, Darlehnsbetrag').
government borrowing

corporate borrowing Kreditaufnahme durch Firmen
heavy borrowing

a borrower ist eine Person oder Institution, die Schulden, Darlehn aufnimmt.
Italy is the biggest borrower in the EC, though its public deficit as a percentage of GDP is not as big as Greece's.
a net borrower Nettoschuldner
the world's largest borrower

cost, cost, cost Verb. Das Verb *cost* ‚(einen Betrag) kosten' wird immer mit Ergänzungen konstruiert.
This has cost a fortune.
workers who cost only $ 1.00 an hour
Both cost the same.
How much should capital cost?
The schemes cost money.

cost Substantiv. Das Substantiv *cost* ‚Kosten' wird im Singular und im Plural verwendet. *cost* kann im Sinne von ‚Preis für etwas' verwendet werden.
an energy tax on the cost of fuel
the cost of water

In der Kombination *the cost of* ... ist häufig von Kapital, Leistungen oder Gesamtkosten allgemeiner Art die Rede.
the cost of capital
the cost of equity
the cost of labour
the cost of maintenance Instandhaltungskosten
the cost of living Lebenshaltungskosten

Wenn von den Kosten gesprochen wird, die eine bestimmte Maßnahme oder Handlung mit sich bringen, kann man das mit *the costs of* plus Verb plus *-ing* (oder *of* mit Substantiv) formulieren.
the costs of cutting inflation
the costs of investing in this project
the costs of reducing greenhouse gases ... um die Treibhausgase zu verringern

Kosten, die sich aus einer Reihe von Posten zusammensetzen, sind *costs*. Jemandes *costs* sind daher die Ausgaben, die für die Führung eines Haushalts oder für die Existenz eines Betriebes anfallen.

social costs Sozialkosten
labour costs Lohnkosten
wage costs Lohngemeinkosten
fixed costs feste Kosten
direct costs Einzelkosten

Bei Verbindungen mit *cost* als erstem Element steht *cost*.
cost curve
cost savings Kosteneinsparungen
cost-cutting
cost-benefit analysis Kosten-Nutzen-Analyse

Entstehen jemandem Kosten, wird *cost to* verwendet.
at a huge cost to its economy
an enormous cost to the public purse

In einigen Wendungen steht *cost*.
at the cost of slower growth mit dem Nachteil von langsamerem Wachstum

Verben mit *costs* als Objekt: *avoid, cover, curb, cut, estimate, force down, impose on, increase, involve, keep down, quantify, raise.*

Das Adjektiv *costly* ist ‚mit relativ hohen Kosten verbunden'.
costly excess capacity teure Überkapazität

credit. Im Zusammenhang mit Geldbeschaffung, Banken kommt *credit* im Sinne von ‚Kredit' vor.
consumer credit Verbraucherkredit
private sector credit growth
short-term/long-term credit
standby credit Beistandskredit
credit market
credit risk

Das Wort *credit* wird aber, im Sinne von ‚Kredit, Darlehen', kaum zusammen mit dem unbestimmten Artikel *a* gebraucht. Stattdessen steht *a loan* (siehe *loan* in diesem Abschnitt).
Der Plural *credits* wird gelegentlich verwendet.
Moscow offered India arms at low prices, as well as cheap credits.

In Verbindung mit Steuer kann ein *credit* ein Freibetrag oder eine sonstige Vergünstigung sein.

tax credit Steuervergünstigung
earned income tax credit (EITC) Steuergutschrift bei niedrigem Arbeitseinkommen
Wenn man sagt, jemand sei *credited with something* oder *deserves the credit for doing something*, dann rechnet man dieser Person etwas als Verdienstleistung an.
‚Kreditwürdigkeit' ist *creditworthiness*.

creditor. *a creditor* ist ein Gläubiger.
senior creditors bevorrechtigte Gläubiger
junior creditors ungesicherte Gläubiger
the world's biggest creditor nation
a net international creditor

debt. *a debt* [det] ist eine zu zahlende Schuld. Wie auch im Deutschen (Schuld – Schulden) gibt es ein Nebeneinander von *debt – debts*.
Poland's crushing debts Polens erdrückende Schulden

Das Wort *debt* wird aber im allgemeinen als Singularwort verwendet, ohne den unbestimmten Artikel *a*.
government debt
public debt
public-sector debt
the national debt
crippled by foreign debt durch Auslandsschulden kaum handlungsfähig
debt burden Schuldenlast
debt-to-GDP-ratio Verhältnis der Gesamtverschuldung zum Bruttosozialprodukt

a debtor ['detə] ist ein Schuldner. Siehe *creditor* in diesem Abschnitt.
a net debtor

indebted (als Adjektiv) ist ‚verschuldet'.
indebted customers
highly-indebted government

Hierzu das Substantiv *indebtedness* ‚Verschuldung'.

expenditure. *expenditure* [ɪk'spendɪtʃə] bezeichnet Kosten, Ausgaben, insbesondere im investiven Bereich. Ein Plural ist möglich, wenn es ausdrücklich um verschiedene Finanzposten geht.

capital expenditure Kapitalaufwand
public expenditure öffentliche Ausgaben
government expenditures Staatsausgaben

expense. *expense* kann als Singularwort (ohne den unbestimmten Artikel *an*) oder mit *an* und auch im Plural verwendet werden. Es kann im Sinne von ‚Ausgaben, Kosten' verwendet werden.
medical expenses
a statement of income and expenses

Unter *expenses* versteht man auch die Betriebskosten, siehe auch den vorhergehenden Eintrag *expenditure*. Ein *expense account* ist ein Spesenkonto. Jemandes *expenses* sind die Spesen, die eine Person macht oder abrechnet.

Die Wendung *at someone's expense* bedeutet entweder ‚so, dass jemand dafür zahlen muss' oder ‚so, dass jemand/etwas einen Nachteil davon hat'.
at the expense of Americans and other foreigners
at the expense of macroeconomic stability

invest. *invest* ‚investieren' kann alleine verwendet werden. Oder mit einer beliebigen Kombination von Objekt (dem Betrag), einer adverbialen Bestimmung (wie *heavily*) und einer Ergänzung mit *in* (worin investiert wird).
the willingness to invest
Developing countries have been investing around $200 billion a year.
When companies invest in a new plant ...
Emerging economies need to invest heavily in infrastructure.

investment. Im Sinne von ‚das Investieren' (dem Akt, der Handlung des Einbringens von Geld) wird *investment* als Singularwort verwendet, ohne den unbestimmten Artikel *an*.
changes in saving and investment
a shift in saving and investment
investment in infrastructure

Verbindungen mit *investment* als erstem Element haben die Singularform.
investment bank
investment company
investment credits
investment demand

investment funds
investment managers
investment opportunities
investment strategy

Eine bestimmte investierte Summe oder investierte Beträge sind dagegen *an investment* bzw. *investments*. Ebenfalls als *an investment/investments* kann ‚angelegtes Geld' bezeichnet werden.
There is every reason to undertake investments that yield the highest returns.
the riskiness of their investments
The returns on an investment must be high enough ...

Der Bereich, in den investiert wird, wird mit *in* angeschlossen. Der Investierende wird mit *by* eingeführt.
the results of investments in health and education
foreign investment in shares
investment by domestic and foreign firms
investment by banks and pension funds

investors. *investors* sind die Investoren.
investors in these markets Personen/Institutionen, die in diese Märkte investieren

lend, lent, lent. *lend* ist das Geben von Geld in Form von Krediten, Darlehen. Das Verb kann für sich alleine gebraucht werden, mit adverbialer Bestimmung, mit direktem und indirektem Objekt (oder mit einem der beiden Objekte).
their ability to lend
British building societies can now raise money on the capital markets ..., making it easier to lend at fixed rates.
banks and others that had lent the firm money
the difficulties facing financial institutions that lent to property developers ... die Geld an Bauträger verliehen haben

Wie bei *borrow* wird häufig das Substantiv (*lending*) gebraucht, als ‚Gewährung von Krediten usw.'
borrowing and lending
reckless lending

Der Gebende ist *the lender*.
a mortgage lender

liability. *liability* beschreibt den Zustand, in dem man zur Rückzahlung von Schulden oder zu Schadenersatz verpflichtet ist. *a liability* ist eine bestimmte Schuld an Geld, auch ein Wort für das Gesamt an Schulden, die jemand hat.

liabilities sind die Schulden, die ein Betrieb bei seinen Gläubigern hat; allgemein auch Geld, das zu zahlen jemand verpflichtet ist.

current liabilities kurzfristige Verbindlichkeiten
deferred tax liabilities aufgeschobene Steuerverbindlichkeiten
pension liabilities Rentenverpflichtungen

assets and liabilities Aktiva und Passiva

Wird von einer Person gesagt, sie sei *a liability (for the company)*, dann ist diese Person eine Gefahr für das Unternehmen.

loan. *a loan* ist ein Darlehen. Ein Darlehen an jemanden ist *a loan to somebody*.
fixed-rate loans mit festen Zinsen
adjustable-rate loans mit variablen Zinsen
loans to property developers
bank loan Bankdarlehen
to authorise a new loan
a cheap loan

mortgage. *a mortgage* ['mɔːgɪdʒ] ist eine Hypothek.
a mortgage bank
mortgage rates
fixed-rate mortgages
mortgage repayments
first mortgage Ersthypothek

Eine Hypothek auf einem Gebäude oder Grundstück ist *a mortgage on* ... Der Geldgebende ist der *mortgagee* [mɔːgɪdʒiː], der Empfangende der *mortgagor*. *to mortgage something* ist ‚etwas mit einer Hypothek belasten'.

owe. Das Verb *owe* wird in formelleren wirtschaftlichen Texten nicht wie in der Gemeinsprache verwendet (wie in *He owed me five dollars*). Wenn es auftritt, dann in der Bedeutung ‚verdanken, eine Folge sein von etwas'.
The growth in self-employment during the 1980s owed more to rising unemployment than to a sudden blossoming of the entrepreneurial spirit. ... war eher eine

Folge der steigenden Arbeitslosigkeit als eines plötzlichen Erwachens unternehmerischer Haltung.

pay, paid, paid Verb. *pay something* ist ‚eine Geldsumme/Zinssatz zahlen'
Central banks have to pay a higher rate of interest.
Firms found to be cheating would have to refund the subsidy and pay a fine. ... würden die Subventionen zurückzahlen und ein Bußgeld zahlen müssen.
people's willingness to pay money
to pay (a sum of money) for something ‚ist für etwas (einen Betrag) bezahlen'.
to pay for a permit
using public money to pay for private schools

Jemandem etwas zahlen ist *pay something to someone* oder *to pay someone something.*
Another idea is to pay more generous benefits to people in work.
If employers are made to pay low-paid workers bigger wages ...

Einen gewissen Anteil für etwas zahlen ist *pay (a sum of money) towards something.*
They should then be asked how much they would be willing to pay towards these programmes in the form of higher prices or taxes.

price. *the price* ist der Preis, die Kosten. ‚Preis von' wird mit *of* konstruiert. *price* wird dabei in Verbindung mit kaufbaren „Objekten" gebraucht, selten in Verbindungen mit Leistungen oder Dienstleistungen.
the price of oil
the price of orange juice

Wenn speziell ausgedrückt werden soll, dass der Preis für etwas bezahlt oder verlangt wird, steht auch *for.*
the rising prices for energy and raw materials
10% of the ticket price for flights within Europe

In Verbindungen mit *price* als zweitem Element bezeichnet der erste Teil das Produkt, für das der Preis gilt oder den Bereich des Preises.
gold prices
milk prices
oil prices
water prices
commodity prices Preise an der Warenbörse

consumer prices Verbraucherpreise
market prices Marktpreise
producer prices Erzeugerpreise
raw material prices Rohstoffpreise
retail prices Einzelhandelspreise

Die Fügung *prices of* ... wird nicht verwendet. Man spricht entweder über *oil prices* oder über *the oil price* (seltener) oder über *the price of oil*.

Mit *price* als erstem Element: *price change, price control, price cuts, price difference, price distortion* (-verzerrung), *price index, price level, price movements, price rise, price signal, price stability, price war*.

Adjektiv plus *price(s)*: *comparable, domestic* (Inlands-), *falling, final* (End-), *high(er), low(er), rising*.

Preise können *adjust* (sich anpassen), *change, collapse, drop, fall, increase, plunge* (abstürzen), *recover, reflect costs, be raised, rise, stabilise, soar, tumble*.

price(s) als Objekt: *cut, curb* (eindämmen), *estimate, keep up* (aufrechterhalten), *monitor* (überwachen), *push up, raise, reduce, set* (festsetzen, bestimmen).

raise. Im Zusammenhang mit Finanzmitteln bedeutet *raise* ‚beschaffen, besorgen'.
Building societies can now raise money on the capital markets.
American firms can raise capital more cheaply than their Japanese counterparts.

LITTLE – SMALL

little. Das Adjektiv *little* wird vor Substantiven gebraucht, die im Singular und ohne den unbestimmten Artikel *a* verwendet werden.
little capital
little cause for concern
with little effect on growth
very little food
little hope
This has little impact on growth. ... geringe Wirkung ...
of little use

a little wird als adverbiale Bestimmung gebraucht, ‚ein wenig'.
In Japan it [annual broad-money growth] rose a little, to 2.4%.
Sao Paulo recovered a little from lows caused by banking worries.
If he cuts the wage a little, he does not lose all of his workers.
They simply make its findings a little crude.
a little prudential supervision (schon) ein geringes Maß an umsichtiger Überwachung

Es tritt auch zusammen mit *above, below, over, under* auf, ‚ein wenig über, unter usw.'
a little over a third of a worker's previous earnings
a little above 14%

Es gibt auch das Adverb *little*, dies bedeutet nicht ‚ein wenig', sondern ‚nur wenig'.
Imports were little changed.
a deficit of $4 billion, little changed from the previous year

In einigen Fällen ist *little* ein Pronomen.
Americans have learnt little. ... haben wenig gelernt.
Chief executives gained little from higher share prices. ... hatten wenig (Gewinn) ...

by little ist ‚um nur wenig'.
The surplus fell by little in dollar terms.

In einigen Wendungen wird *little* gebraucht.
In practice the motive behind much aid has had little to do with helping the poor.
... haben die Motive, die der Entwicklungshilfe zugrundeliegen, wenig mit wirklicher Hilfe für die Armen zu tun.
Some economists say that capital inflows have played little part. ... nur eine geringe Rolle gespielt haben.

small. *small* drückt aus, dass jemand oder etwas klein ist, dass etwas nur in geringem Umfang vorhanden ist, dass etwas nur wenig ist. Es kann vor einem Substantiv stehen, nach einem Verb wie *be,* es kann gesteigert werden, es kann modifiziert werden durch Adverbien, wie z.B. *too, quite, relatively*. Als Adverb wird *small* nicht verwendet. Außerdem steht es vor Substantiven, die sowohl eine Singularform als auch eine Pluralform haben.

Only in small countries where foreign aid makes up more than 15% of GDP ...
The gains from trade nearly always look surprisingly small when you try to calculate them.
small firms

a much smaller share of GDP
... while its current-account surplus was also a tad smaller ... ein wenig geringer
... its smallest 12-month rise since July 1989
a relatively small share of its revenues
a small break
a small net outflow
a small rise

Abweichend hiervon ist die Wendung *It is small comfort to* plus Infinitiv ‚Es ist ein geringer Trost zu ... '.

LOSE – LOSS

lose, lost, lost Verb. *lose* [lu:z] ist ‚etwas nicht länger haben und somit einen Verlust erleiden'. *lose* kann für sich gebraucht werden. Es kann durch *from* ergänzt werden.
Farmers will lose. Die Bauern werden (dabei) verlieren.
Developing countries do not lose from the GATT deal. ... bei, durch, an ...

Die häufigsten Objekte zu *lose* sind *competitiveness, confidence, control* (nicht länger beherrschen), *customers, earnings, one's job, interest* (Interesse verlieren), *market share, money, revenues* (Steuerverluste erleiden). Auch Zahlen können Objekte sein.
In trade-weighted terms the dollar gained 2.8% during the week; sterling lost 1.2%.
In Europe Madrid lost 2.0%, Frankfurt 1.9%, Paris 0.8% and London 0.6%.

to lose sleep over something ist ‚größere Sorgen haben'. *to lose ground to someone* ist ‚gegenüber jemandem an Boden verlieren'. Wenn etwas *lost to someone* ist, ist es an jemanden verloren.
Buenos Aires rose by 3.3%, but other Latin American markets lost ground.

loss Substantiv. *loss* ist das Substantiv zu *lose*. Die genauere Art des Verlustes kann durch vorgestelltes Substantiv ausgedrückt werden, auch durch Adjektive.
job loss
real wage losses
real income losses
annual losses
temporary losses

Der Bereich, in dem Verlust entsteht, wird mit *in* eingeführt.
temporary losses in output and employment
the loss in workers' earnings
‚Verlust an' wird mit *of* konstruiert, ebenso der Verlust ‚in Höhe von'.
the loss of revenue from VAT rückläufiges Mehrwertsteueraufkommen
the loss of tax
a loss of confidence
cumulative losses of $870 billion

Ein Verlust für jemand ist *a loss for someone*, ein Verlust, mit dem jemand fertig werden muss, ist *a loss to someone*.
relative losses for the lower paid
This represented an annual loss to developing countries of $100 billion in 1993.

at a loss ist ‚mit Verlust(en)'.
At current prices of 50 cents a lb, two-fifths of all zinc mines are operating at a loss.
... mit Verlusten

-LY-ADVERBIEN

In diesem Abschnitt wird auf einen besonderen Gebrauch von Adverbien hingewiesen. Es handelt sich um solche, die auf *-ly* enden, am Anfang eines Satzes oder Nebensatzes stehen und (fast immer) von einem Komma gefolgt werden.
Clearly, it is good to test whether the unemployed really want to work.

Sie werden verwendet um auszudrücken, dass das Folgende ‚in ... Hinsicht', ‚aus Sicht von ...' gilt oder aufzufassen ist.
Socially, this will be explosive. Das wird sozialen Zündstoff geben.
Politically, this is a far trickier option. Politisch gesehen ist das eine wesentlich kompliziertere Lösung.

Zu diesem Typ gehören weiterhin z.B. *geographically, technologically, psychologically, historically, financially.*

Solche Adverbien werden auch verwendet, um die persönliche Einschätzung des Folgenden auszudrücken, also ‚es ist, nach meiner Meinung ... so, dass'.
Sadly, the OECD's answer is no. Leider ...
Clearly, cutting down some trees and burning some scarce natural gas is all right. Es leuchtet ein, dass ...

Curiously, far less attention has been paid to the significance of changes in commercial-property prices. Es ist merkwürdig, dass ...
Oddly, the minimum-wage idea is a lot more popular. Seltsamerweise/Seltsam, aber ...

Zu diesem Typ gehören weiterhin
actually in Wirklichkeit
inevitably es ist unvermeidbar
fortunately zum Glück
plainly offensichtlich
possibly
strikingly es überrascht sehr, dass/es ist sehr auffällig, dass
surprisingly es überrascht, dass
surely sicherlich
unfortunately leider
unsurprisingly wie zu erwarten
typically typisch, wie zu erwarten.

Mit einigen der *ly*-Adverbien wird eine Art sprachlicher Kommentar zum Folgenden gegeben, etwas wird auf eine bestimmte Weise formuliert.
Briefly, the argument runs as follows. Kurz gesagt, ...

Dazu auch *broadly/generally* (*speaking*) ‚allgemein gesprochen'. Hierzu kann man auch diejenigen *ly*-Adverbien stellen, die sich auf die Gliederung des Textes beziehen, vor allem *finally/lastly* ‚zum Schluss'.

Einige Adverbien auf *-ably* können mit ‚man kann' plus Verb umschrieben werden:
arguably man kann argumentieren
conceivably man kann sich vorstellen

Adverbien auf *-edly* implizieren ‚es ist ..., dass'
admittedly es ist zuzugeben, dass

Schließlich gibt es einige Adverbien der Zeit, die häufig am Satzanfang stehen, wie *occasionally, recently, usually.*

MANY – MUCH

many ist ‚viele'. Das folgende Substantiv muss ein Pluralwort sein. ‚viel mehr' vor einem Substantiv im Plural ist *many more*.

Many people do not bother to register as unemployed.
in many developed countries
rapid growth in many Asian economies
the many different kinds of electric light
the many views that Keynes expressed during his lifetime
many more people

Das Pronomen *many* kann für sich als Subjekt stehen (nicht aber als Objekt verwendet werden).
Credit expanded dramatically – and the proportion of bad loans soared. Many were loans to companies linked to the banks themselves.

many steht vor allem dann als Subjekt, wenn ‚viele' einer bestimmten Ansicht sind.
Many argue that foreign aid is a waste of money.
Many believe that ...
Many fear that ...

‚Viele der/von' ist *many of*.
Many of the biggest recipients of aid have enjoyed large inflows of private capital.

many steht zwischen *as ... as*, wenn es sich auf ein vorangehendes Substantiv im Plural (hier: *51 jobs*) bezieht.
For every 1,000 people of working age, America created 51 jobs (net of job losses) in private services, three times as many as in France or western Germany.

much. Im Sinne von ‚viel' steht *much* vor solchen Substantiven, die keine Pluralform und auch nicht den unbestimmten Artikel *a* haben können.
But they are unlikely to pay much attention.
In practice the motive behind much aid has had little to do with helping the poor.
More fundamentally, some people are questioning whether aid actually does much good.

Das *much* kann ein *more* vor dem Substantiv verstärken, ‚viel mehr, weitaus mehr'.
France's former African colonies receive much more aid than their equally poor neighbours.

much als Adverb bedeutet ‚viel', insbesondere zusammen mit dem Verb *cost*.
Industrial electricity costs almost twice as much as in Japan.
Long-term interests have not fallen as much as short-term interests.

much of steht vor *the*, vor einer *'s*-Form (und vor *it, this, that* und Nebensätzen mit *what*).

... *much of East Asia's recent economic success* ...
much of what was sold in January

Dieses *much of* geht auch mit Zeiträumen.
during much of the 1980s

much kann alleine als Subjekt stehen, ‚viel/vieles'.
Much depends on the indicators used to measure their welfare.

Vor Adjektiven und Adverbien im Komparativ ist *much* ‚viel'.
America's yield curve is sloping upwards much more steeply than a year ago.
Japanese companies, however, have focused much more on Asia.
In non-European G7 countries (with the exception of Canada) the state accounts for a much smaller share of GDP than it does in Europe.
a much bigger problem
much less influential
It has made banks much more cautious about lending.

Adjektive, die auf *-ed* enden, können ein *much* haben.
a much-used explanation ... eine oft verwendete Erklärung.

In Verbindung mit dem Superlativ ist *much the* ‚weitaus'.
But they are still much the biggest source of new capital.

much als Adverb kann in der Vergleichsstruktur *as ... as* stehen.
A dollar invested at 10% will be worth six times as much a century from now as a dollar invested at 8%.
Does Japan import as much as it ought to?

how much ist ‚wie viel', *so much* ‚so viel'. ‚So viel zum Problem x' ist *So much for* ...
So much for the market's supposed foresight.

Mit *much as* wird gesagt, dass etwas in ziemlich ähnlicher Weise der Fall ist.
Much as the microeconomists predicted.
much as in Europe wie ganz ähnlich in Europa

MAY – MIGHT

Wie *can, could, must, should* und andere sind *may* und *might* Modalverben. Die meisten Modalverben schränken das Gesagte so ein, dass es nicht als tatsächlich dargestellt wird.

may. *may* bedeutet, dass etwas vielleicht oder möglicherweise der Fall ist, dass etwas so sein kann oder könnte.
Even this may be too optimistic. Selbst das ist vielleicht zu optimistisch.
That may be one reason why ... Das ist möglicherweise ein Grund, warum ...
That may cause friction. Das führt vielleicht zu Konflikten.

Die Möglichkeit auf die *may* verweist ist eine etwas andere als die von *can*. Es liegt sozusagen im Wesen von Preisen, dass sie steigen oder fallen (können): *Prices can rise or fall* – eine prinzipielle Möglichkeit. Dagegen liegt mit *Prices may rise* eine aktuelle gegenwärtige Möglichkeit oder durchaus denkbare zukünftige Möglichkeit vor. Daher ist *may* in der Regel mit ‚vielleicht', ‚es ist möglich, dass', ‚könnte' zu übersetzen (und nicht mit ‚kann, können').

may kann durch *well* ‚durchaus' verstärkt werden.
America may well be able to impose its will.

Die angesprochene abgeschwächte Tatsächlichkeit führt zu einer Reihe von Formeln, mit denen die Verbindlichkeit reduziert wird.
It may be better to ...
That may be true.
That may seem true.
It may be possible to ...
They may be right.
This may seem perverse.
This may seem/sound good.
But this may be not easy.
That may not necessarily be the case.

Eine wichtige Bedeutung von *may* ist die, dass etwas „zwar" nicht unrichtig ist oder scheint, dass aber dennoch das andere Behauptete eher zutrifft – eine Art Einräumung. Diese Bedeutung von *may* findet sich in der Umgebung von *although, though, yet, but* und ähnlichen. Beachte das *partly right* im zweiten der folgenden Beispiele.
It may seem intuitively appealing that rich countries should give money to poorer ones to help them grow faster and live better. Yet the economic logic behind this notion is surprisingly weak. Es erscheint zwar ... Doch die wirtschaftliche Logik, die dieser Vorstellung zugrunde liegt ...
At first sight, it may seem that competition policy is merely the latest stick used by American trade negotiators to beat the Japanese. Although that view is partly right ...

Die allgemeinsprachliche Bedeutung ‚dürfen' von *may* ist in wirtschaftlichen Texten sehr selten (wie überhaupt selten von „Erlaubnis" die Rede ist.) Beachte, dass die Verben *allow* und *permit* vorwiegend im Sinne von ‚ermöglichen' verwendet werden.

may kann verwendet werden um zu sagen, dass etwas unter Umständen der Fall ist und irgendwie genutzt werden kann.
the value a forest may have as a home for wildlife or a place for recreation

may have und Partizip Perfekt. Damit wird formuliert, dass etwas in der Vergangenheit möglich war (sich aber nicht ereignet hat), ferner, dass es möglich ist, dass etwas in der Vergangenheit so war.
Past attempts to use monetary policy to create jobs may have had some effect in the short term. Die Versuche in der Vergangenheit, durch Geldpolitik Arbeitsplätze zu schaffen, hatten vielleicht Erfolg, kurzfristig.
The latest cut in German interest rates by the Bundesbank may have helped to ease tensions between the leaders of EC countries.
Once, British journalists may have been better educated than Americans ... Es ist möglich, dass britische Journalisten in der Vergangenheit eine bessere Ausbildung hatten als amerikanische ...

Diese Konstruktion kann sich auch auf die Zukunft beziehen.
By then governments may have woken up to a yet more radical option. Zu diesem Zeitpunkt werden die Regierungen reagieren und sich radikaleren Überlegungen stellen müssen.

might. Wie *may* kann auch *might* bedeuten, dass etwas vielleicht oder möglicherweise der Fall ist, dass etwas so sein kann oder sein könnte. Wie *may* kann auch *might* mit *even* oder *well* kombiniert werden.
The money might be used in half-a-dozen ways.
Different models might even co-exist side by side. Verschiedene Modelle könnten sogar nebeneinander bestehen.
Higher consumption might well be a goal in itself. Höherer Konsum könnte sehr wohl ein Ziel für sich selbst sein.

Häufiger als *may* wird *might* beim Argumentieren verwendet: es könnte zwar so sein – aber es ist nicht so/anderes ist wichtiger.
Does this mean that organised corruption might be harmless or even beneficial? Almost certainly not.
Many might argue that life is priceless. But governments must – and do – put monetary values on life and limb.

Mit *might have* und Partizip der Vergangenheit wird ausgedrückt, dass etwas in der Vergangenheit möglich war (sich aber nicht ereignet hat).
America might have abandoned the Uruguay round. ... hätte verlassen können.

America might not have insisted on it ist ‚Amerika hätte vielleicht nicht darauf bestanden', d.h., es ist möglich, dass etwas nicht der Fall gewesen war. *America could not have insisted on it* hingegen ist ‚Amerika hätte nicht darauf bestehen können', d.h., es war unmöglich, dass etwas der Fall war.

MONEY – MONETARY

Einige der häufigen Verbindungen mit *money* sind
money aggregates Geldmengen (M1, M2, M3)
money demand
money expenditure
money market Geldmarkt
money income
money policy
money supply Geldmenge

money market selbst hat weitere Kombinationen, dann in der Form *money-market (assistance, operations, rates, yield curve)*. Die Verbindungen mit *money* beziehen sich meist auf *money* im Sinne von ‚Geldsumme, Geldbetrag', nur selten auf *money* im Sinne von ‚Währung'.
Hingegen bezieht sich das Adjektiv *monetary* in einer Reihe von Fügungen auf Währung.
International Monetary Fund IMF
Economic and Monetary Union EMU
monetary policy
the European monetary system
the monetary base Zentralbankgeldmenge

Allerdings gibt es *monetary policy* neben *money policy, monetary growth* neben *money growth* ‚Geldzuwachs'. In Einzelfällen empfiehlt sich daher das Nachschlagen.

PLANEN UND BEABSICHTIGEN

Siehe hierzu auch die Abschnitte ERWARTEN, SCHÄTZEN, VORAUSSAGEN und GEFAHREN, PROBLEME, SCHWIERIGKEITEN.
Zu den Modalverben *can/could, may/might, shall/should, will/would* siehe die entsprechenden Abschnitte CAN – COULD, MAY – MIGHT, SHOULD – OUGHT TO, WILL – WOULD.

agree. Im Sinne von ‚zustimmen' kann *agree* alleine gebraucht werden.
It is not certain that Israel will agree.
Mr Baumol agrees.

Die Sache, der zugestimmt wird kann mit *to* oder *on* eingeführt werden.
Governments are unlikely to agree on any such measures in Washington.
No two economists agree either on how to adjust the deficit for the cycle or indeed on what 'the deficit' actually is.
to agree to a deal
Andreotti's four-party government agreed to budget cuts of 55 trillion lire.
... what has already been agreed upon. ... worüber bereits Einigung erzielt worden ist.
But suppose new managers feel no obligation to honour merely implicit contracts agreed to by their predecessors.

Zusammen mit einem *that*-Satz ist *agree* ‚derselben Meinung sein'.
Nearly all economists agree that the Russian rouble is undervalued.

Dieses *that* kann weggelassen werden.
[They] agreed their job had become much tougher.

agree to do something drückt die Bereitschaft aus, etwas zu tun.
The Japanese agreed to improve foreign access to their flat-glass market.

to agree something ist ‚einig werden in Bezug auf, akzeptieren', vor allem in Hinblick auf Preise und Standards.
This helps explain why it is often so difficult for groups of firms to agree a standard among themselves.
The television industry may never be able to agree an HDTV standard.
This increase in the IMF's resources ... was agreed by the IMF's board of governors a year ago.

Einige Formeln mit *agree* können zwischen Kommas gesetzt werden.

The treaty on EMU will, it is agreed, forbid the EuroFed, or national central banks, to provide finance to any government.
Especially important, we agree, is ...

Das Partizip *agreed* kann, zusammen mit Adverb, als Adjektiv verwendet werden.
the newly agreed world climate treaty das kürzlich vereinbarte Weltklimaabkommen...

aim Verb. *aim at/for something* und *aim to do something* werden in der Bedeutung ‚beabsichtigen, etwas zu ereichen' verwendet.
There are two sorts of FDI: that which chases cheaper resources such as labour, capital and raw materials; and that aimed at access to markets.
America should aim for a budget surplus.
The best treaty will aim for the smallest loss in world welfare.
The EC's heads of government aim to prepare the way for economic and monetary union (EMU).
... Taiwan's exporters, aiming to offset America's growing share of their market ...

Wenn etwas *aimed at someone* ist, dann ist es auf jemanden abgezielt, abgestimmt, an jemanden gerichtet.
... 4,700 share-option schemes aimed mostly at executives.

aim Substantiv. *an aim* ist das, was man zu erreichen beabsichtigt. *aim* wird vorzugsweise mit *to* und Infinitv angeschlossen, oder mit *of.* Zwischen *aim, goal, purpose* besteht in der Bedeutung kein größerer Unterschied, allerdings werden diese Wörter jeweils anders konstruiert, siehe die betreffenden Einträge in diesem Abschnitt.
The declared aim is to prevent a future rise in inflation.
Its aim is to improve company decision-making.
The aim of this grander scheme was to enable policy-makers to combine stability in real exchange rates with steady, non-inflationary growth.

choose, chose, chosen Verb. Die übliche Gleichsetzung von *choose* und ‚wählen' ist nicht korrekt. Mit nachfolgendem *to* und Infinitiv bedeutet *choose* ‚sich entscheiden, etwas zu tun'.
The American subsidiaries of Japanese firms usually choose to raise finance in the American domestic market.

Firms can choose to supply an overseas market either by exporting to it or by locating production there.

In allen anderen Verwendungen bedeutet *choose,* dass man aus zwei oder mehreren Möglichkeiten eine davon aussucht, auswählt, sich für eine entscheidet.
Britons and New Zealanders can choose their telephone company.
Parents [can] choose between public and private schools.
French car buyers can choose from around 700 models made by 60 manufacturers.

choice. *choice* (im Singular) ist das Substantiv zu *choose* und kann prinzipiell ‚Möglichkeit der Auswahl' bedeuten.
... but consumers suffer because their choice is deliberately limited.
Any producer has a wide choice of how to sell his goods.

choice about something ist ein Spielraum bei Entscheidungen.
Mostly, managers may have some choice about when to invest.

Die (Aus-)Wahl zwischen verschiedenen Dingen ist *the choice between things.*
... to ensure that parents have a choice between different types of schools.

Wenn Auswahlmöglichkeiten vorliegen, kann *a choice* eine Entscheidung sein.
[They] will need to make some exceptionally difficult economic choices.
This could pose an awkward choice for the Bank of Japan.
... consumers can rationally make bad choices.
a 75% probability of making the right choice ... die richtige Entscheidung zu treffen

decide. Mit *decide* wird ausgedrückt, dass man etwas bestimmt oder dass man sich entscheidet, etwas zu tun.
Mit direktem Objekt ist die Bedeutung ‚bestimmen/sich entscheiden, dass etwas irgendwie ist oder wird'.
In some cases economists can decide their worth indirectly.
Students of the subject are trained to regard self-interest as the force that decides economic choices.

‚sich zwischen etwas entscheiden' wird mit *decide between* ausgedrückt.
You must decide between two road-safety schemes.

Wenn man zu dem Entschluss kommt, dass sich etwas irgendwie verhält, wird mit einem *that*-Satz ergänzt.
Mr Mieno may simply have decided that it was safe to cut interest rates.

This is why European countries decided in the 1980s that tying their currencies tightly to the inflation-proof D-mark was the best way to beat inflation.
Die Entscheidung, etwas zu tun, hat die Konstruktion *to* plus Infinitiv, oder mit einem *wh*-Satz, also einem Satz, der mit *when, whether, where, how* usw. beginnt.
If American politicians were to decide to switch to the German model ...
The Bundesbank decided not to cut interest rates.
The FCC controls private-sector broadcasting rights by deciding which companies will have access to the limited number of radio-spectrum bands available.
It is then up to governments to decide whether, and how, to use some of the gains to compensate the losers.

decision. *decision* ist das Substantiv zu *decide*.
To make rational decisions, governments must have some idea of the off-setting benefits. ... vernünftige Entscheidungen ...
The decisions of the first few consumers of a product can determine its fate. Die Einschätzung eines Produkts durch die ersten Verbraucher ...
decisions taken in secret by civil servants
An independent bank would have to make inescapably political decisions about the rate at which inflation should be brought down.
his recent decision to build a new factory
the Fed's recent decision to raise interest rates
Das Sich-Entscheiden, Sich-Entschließen ist *decision-making*.

design. *to design something* ist ‚etwas (auch in Einzelheiten) planen, entwerfen.'
Der Unterschied zu *to plan* ist vor allem, dass bei *to plan* häufig ‚Planwirtschaft, zentrale Planung (im abschätzigen Sinne)' assoziiert ist.
a tool for designing regulations
poorly designed auctions
a well-designed energy tax
The commission therefore designed a tax ...

‚geplant als' ist *designed as.*
The ERM was originally designed as a multilateral system of currencies.
Als Passivkonstruktion mit *to* plus Infinitiv ist die Bedeutung ‚sollen, beabsichtigt sein'.
North American free trade, likewise, is designed to bring political openness to Mexico.

Continental Europe is riddled with product-market barriers, supposedly designed to preserve existing jobs or to protect the environment.

Das Substantiv zum Verb ist *design (of something)*.
Assembly-process design gives Japan the edge in car-making.
Die Planenden selbst (die „Architekten") sind *designers*.

goal. *a goal* ist ein Ziel, ein Zweck. Mit anschließendem *of* wird die Person/Institution eingeführt, die das Ziel hat, auch die Art des Zieles.
long-term goals langfristige Ziele
a medium-term goal
The prime goal of central banks is to defeat inflation. Das vorrangige Ziel ...
The goal of foreign aid – at least officially – is usually to help the poor.

Ein Ziel verfolgen: *pursue*; erreichen: *achieve, meet*; verfehlen: *miss*; gefährden: *jeopardise* ['dʒepədaɪz]; setzen: *set*.

in order to. *in order to* mit folgendem Infinitiv drückt einen Zweck, eine Absicht aus, ‚um (so) ... zu', ‚damit'. Es steht meist am Ende des Satzes und kann durch Kommas abgetrennt werden. Es ist gleichbedeutend mit der Konstruktion *to* plus Infinitiv und wird vor allem dann eingesetzt, wenn die letztgenannte Konstruktion mehrdeutig sein könnte.
France is committed to a strong franc, in order to keep down inflation.
This [tax] would be levied on the carbon content of fossil fuels in order to reduce the rate at which carbon dioxide ... is building up in the atmosphere.
Japan is being forced to run an excessively tight monetary policy in order to keep the yen high to please the American government.

intend. *intend* ‚beabsichtigen' wird mit *to* und Infinitiv oder einem *that*-Satz ergänzt. Passivformen sind häufig; die Bedeutung ist dann ‚sollen/vorsehen, dass/ zum Ziel haben'.
[These measures] are intended to keep the 1992 budget deficit to the target agreed earlier this year. ... sollen das Haushaltsdefizit ...
That law bans any agreement between firms intended to prevent or distort competition. ... Vereinbarungen zwischen Firmen, aufgrund derer der Wettbewerb verhindert oder verzerrt werden sollte.

Last month the Greek parliament passed a law intended to stop self-employed people under-reporting their incomes to the taxman.
It is intended that this overfunding will be offset in the new financial year.
Das Partizip *intended* kann als Adjektiv verwendet werden.
the intended or past acquisition of US-based corporations

intent Adjektiv. Wenn man *intent on doing something* ist, ist man fest entschlossen, etwas zu tun.
This leaves plenty of unfinished business for governments still intent on reducing spending. ... die immer noch fest entschlossen sind, die Ausgaben zu reduzieren.

intention. *an intention* ist eine Absicht.
The intention is not to replace the SNA ...

intention wird mit *to* und Infinitiv oder mit *of* und der *-ing*-Form des Verbs ergänzt.
his declared intention of turning management into a discipline akin to the physical sciences seine erklärte Absicht, Management zu einer Disziplin ähnlich den Naturwissenschaften zu machen

like Verb. *like to do something* bedeutet, dass man etwas gerne bzw. öfters tut.
American firms like to complain about cut-throat Japanese competition.
Governments like to blame their budget deficits on the economic downturn.
a monopolist that would like to stop entry into its market

plan Verb. *plan* mit Objekt bedeutet, dass man etwas Zukünftiges mehr oder weniger genau umreißt.
History suggests that few lasting financial innovations have been planned.
No football coach plans an attack without taking into account the defenders' likely response.

plan mit *to* und Infinitiv ist ‚beabsichtigen'.
[The Ukraine] plans to issue its own currency in due course, and other republics may do the same.

planning und *planned* werden oft verwendet, wenn es um Planwirtschaft geht (aber nicht ausschließlich, siehe drittes Beispiel).
an era of central planning

former centrally planned economies
long-term financial planning

Das Partizip *planned* kann als Adjektiv gebraucht werden.
That is six times the planned figure.

plan Substantiv.

as part of its latest plan to combat inflation Absicht
In the 1980s, it seemed, no self-respecting economics minister was without a plan to deregulate this or that industry.
government-guaranteed company pension plans
Meanwhile Russian politicians pursue their endless debate about which of 64,000 competing plans for economic reform should be adopted. ... Pläne für ...
on current plans nach den gegenwärtigen Plänen

propose. *propose* ist ‚vorschlagen, anregen'.
Many economists are now proposing a radical solution.
We did propose, however, that such pressure should meet two tests.

Das Partizip *proposed* kann als Adjektiv verwendet werden.
under their proposed scheme

Das Substantiv zu *propose* ist *proposal.*
The current proposals are unclear.
... a proposal to tie the dollar, yen and D-mark together in a system of exchange-rate target zones.

(*a proposition* ist eine Ansicht oder eine Theorie.)

purpose. *purpose* ist ‚Zweck, Ziel'. Das Wort wird häufig mit *for* kombiniert: ‚zum Zweck von/für ... Ziele'
Yet for policy purposes, it hardly matters which is the more important.
For all practical purposes the state-owned banking system is bankrupt ... ist das staatseigene Bankensystem praktisch bankrott
for this purpose zu diesem Zweck/um das zu erreichen
Government borrowing can serve the purpose of smoothing tax rates over time. ... dient dazu ...
An auction, therefore, tries to serve two purposes. ... versucht, zwei Ziele zu erreichen.

seek, sought, sought. Mit *seek* wird die Absicht oder der Versuch ausgedrückt, etwas zu bekommen (*seek something*) oder etwas zu tun (*seek to do something*). Es wird häufig im Umfeld von Arbeit, Jobs, Problemen, Lösungen verwendet.
the incentive to seek work
a flood of unemployed workers seeking jobs in the West
Economists have long sought ways to make the labour market work better.
As the wage falls, firms seek to employ more workers.
All are seeking to survive and prosper.
The 'new interventionism' seeks to guide, not replace, the market.

Einige Bildungen mit *seek* werden öfters gebraucht: *a job-seeker, a profit-seeker, a bribe-seeker, an asylum seeker.*

scheme. *a scheme* [ski:m] ist ein (meist größerer) Plan, die Ausarbeitungen von Vorstellungen, wie etwas funktionieren könnte.
In the Williamson scheme, internal balance is more easily achieved.
Under Mr Snower's scheme ...

a scheme ist auch ein Modell, nach dem vorgegangen wird, ein System. Die Art des Systems oder Modells wird durch vorangehende Substantive beschrieben.
the national pension scheme
employee share-ownership schemes
health-care schemes
a job-subsidy scheme

***to*-Infinitiv**. Am Satzanfang hat ein Infinitiv mit *to* und einem folgenden Komma die Bedeutung ‚um ... zu, zum Zweck des ...'.
To test this, Mr Boone tries to measure the direct effect of foreign aid on indicators of human development.
To determine the relative importance of these barriers, McKinsey studied selected industries.
To keep inflation in check, policy-makers need a reliable early-warning indicator.

Weitere geläufige Wendungen sind: *to illustrate*, ‚um ein Beispiel zu geben', *to sum up* ‚um zusammenzufassen'.

Diese Konstruktion ist zu trennen von der Folgenden: Hier ist der Infinitiv das Subjekt.
To argue in this way is fair enough. So zu argumentieren ist in Ordnung.

try. *to try something* ist ‚etwas ausprobieren, es mit etwas versuchen'.
Mr. Amihud tried another adjustment.

In der Regel wird *try* mit *to* und Infinitv weitergeführt, ‚versuchen, etwas zu tun'.
Governments should try to catch and punish tax dodgers.
They agreed to try to stabilise the dollar.
Vietnam is trying to become the region's newest dragon.

try hard impliziert große Anstrengungen.
Governments in rich countries try hard to cut spending.

want. *want* ist ‚haben wollen, verlangen', in der Konstruktion *want something*.
Employees want a fixed wage.
Now poorer people want the same choices.
If you want more workers, you go out and hire them.

In der Konstruktion *want to* mit Infinitiv ist es ‚wollen, beabsichtigen'.
They must explain why they want to be different.
If the Fed wants to hold down inflation ...
Governments are unlikely to want to give up control over competition.

Wenn man beabsichtigt, dass etwas irgendwie wird, ist die Konstruktion *want something* plus Adjektiv.
Americans want their dollar free. [nicht an eine andere Währung gebunden]

Beabsichtigt man, dass etwas getan wird: *want something* plus Partizip der Vergangenheit (oder *want something* plus *to be* plus Partizip der Vergangenheit).
They want something done. Sie wollen, dass etwas getan wird.
... those who wanted stage two delayed ... dass die zweite Stufe verzögert würde
Would you want a particular programme to be enacted if you had to pay dollars X for it?

Wenn man möchte oder will, dass jemand etwas tut oder wenn man etwas von einer Sache/Person erwartet, ist die Konstruktion *want somebody/something to do something*.
They have said they want output this year to grow by a mere 9%.
America wants developing countries to comply with the TRIPs agreement more quickly than was agreed in the Uruguay round.

be willing. *be willing to do something* drückt aus, dass die Bereitschaft besteht, etwas zu tun. In den meisten Fällen handelt es sich dabei um eine Bereitschaft zu zahlen oder darum, ein gewisses Risiko einzugehen.
They should then be asked how much they would be willing to pay towards these programmes in the form of higher prices or taxes. Airlines are willing to pay such sums.
Workers will be more willing to take this risk.
Consumers are willing to borrow ...

Wenn die Bereitschaft nicht besteht: *be unwilling to do something.*
Lawyers at Bell Labs were initially unwilling even to apply for a patent. ... waren anfangs nicht einmal bereit ...
If Germany (i.e., the Bundesbank) is unwilling to take responsibility for European economic stability, ...

Die entsprechenden Substantive sind *willingness* bzw. *unwillingness.*
Mr Blinder's willingness to risk a bit more inflation is no surprise.
... people's willingness to pay money to prevent future damage ...

RELATIVSÄTZE

Sätze wie die folgenden enthalten Relativsätze.
1. *Modern game theory was fathered by John von Neumann, a mathematician, and Oskar Morgenstern, an economist, <u>who published 'Theory of Games and Economic Behaviour' in 1944.</u>*
2. *A producer uses only those retailers <u>who agree to support his brand in specified ways.</u>*
3. *Britain is one of the few countries <u>in which the government issues index-linked bonds.</u>*
4. *A company <u>which has developed a particular technology</u> ...*
5. *In Boston, <u>where parents are inundated with information</u>, 57% choose non-local schools ...* wo die Eltern mit Information überschüttet werden ...

Relativsätze werden mit Relativpronomen (wie *which, that, who, whose*) oder anderen Relativwörtern (wie *when, where, how, why*) eingeleitet. Sie geben weitere Information zu dem, was durch das vorangehende Substantiv bezeichnet ist. Diese weitere Information ist von zweierlei Art.

a) Mit der einen Art wird ein Bezug auf eine spezifizierte Untermenge möglich, einer Untermenge zu dem, was durch das Substantiv bezeichnet ist. In Beispiel 2 oben handelt es sich also um ‚solche Einzelhändler, welche ... ‚, in Beispiel 4 um ‚eine solche Firma, welche ... ‚. Man kann auch sagen, dass der Relativsatz zur Identifikation nötig ist.

Solche Relativsätze haben kein Komma vor dem Relativpronomen oder Relativwort. In solchen Relativsätzen kann man statt ... *(retailers) who* ... oder ... *(a company) which* ... auch ... *(retailers/a company) that* ... sagen.

b) Mit der anderen Art der Information wird „nur" zusätzliche, erläuternde Information gegeben. Diese ist für den genauen Bezug, für die genaue Identifikation, nicht erforderlich. Das Boston im Beispiel 5 ist ausreichend. In Beispiel 1 ist mit dem Namen Oskar Morgenstern klar, wer gemeint ist: Die Information *„der 1944 die ‚Theory of Games and Economic Behaviour' veröffentlichte"* ist zwar sinnvoll, aber zur Identifikation nicht erforderlich.

Solche Relativsätze haben ein Komma vor dem Relativpronomen bzw. Relativwort. In solchen Sätzen kann *that* als Relativpronomen nicht stehen.

Relativsätze und Partizipien. Ein Kennzeichen von formeller Sprache sind Konstruktionen, die so aussehen, als seien *which/who/that* und eine Form von *be* „ausgelassen" worden. Gesetzt wird nur das Partizip der Vergangenheit.

The gap widened in 12 of the 17 countries studied. ... in 12 der 17 untersuchten Länder *[which were/have been studied]*
a panel of experts chaired by two Nobel laureates ... unter dem Vorsitz von ... *[... that was chaired by ...]*
examples cited by Mr Nordhaus die von Mr Nordhaus angeführten Beispiele *[... that were cited ...]*

Ähnlich die folgenden Beispiele, bei denen das Relativpronomen ausgelassen ist und das Partizip der Gegenwart für eine Verbform im Präsens steht.
firms remaining at home im Inland verbleibende Firmen
figures ranging between $1m and $4m
products made using processes causing cross-border pollution Produkte, bei deren Herstellung grenzüberschreitende Umweltverschmutzung entsteht
foreigners looking for a regulatory system

Dabei ist besonders zu beachten, dass viele Partizipien nicht, wie im Deutschen, als vorangestellte Adjektive verwendet werden können. ‚Untersuchte Länder' sind eben nicht **studied countries* (sondern *countries studied*), ‚entstandene Verschmutzung eben nicht **caused pollution*. Und ein gerettetes oder erhaltenes Leben ist *a life saved*.

's

Die Konstruktion *X's X* (z.B. *America's exports*) ist zahlenmäßig eine der häufigsten Konstruktionen in finanziellen oder wirtschaftlichen Berichten. Sie kann für verschiedene Ausdruckszwecke eingesetzt werden. Die Konstruktion steht oft in Konkurrenz zu der Fügung mit einem Adjektiv der Nationalität plus X (z.B. *the American currency*). Eine weitere Konkurrenz ergibt sich zwischen z.B. *America's X* und *X in America*. Siehe hierzu in diesem Abschnitt den Hinweis im Eintrag ‚Ort'.

Zeitbestimmungen. Zeitabschnitte wie *this year's, the week's, the previous month's* können Substantiven vorangehen, vor allem in Verbindung mit Superlativen.
But Caracas was the week's biggest loser.
this year's best performing emerging-market equities ...

Zeitangaben im Plural hängen nur ein Apostroph an.
Copper stocks are down to less than six weeks' consumption.

Etwas tun, ausgehen von. Die Konstruktion *X's X* (z.B. *America's exports*) kann ausdrücken, dass jemand etwas getan hat, allgemeiner, dass etwas von etwas ausgeht.
... our panel's forecast of GDP growth [der Panel hat vorausgesagt, dass ...]
the OECD's estimates
the market's concerns

Ort. Häufig zeigt *X's X* (z.B. *Japan's industry*) an, dass es sich um einen Bereich „in" einem Staat oder einer Stadt (bzw. „an" einer Börse) handelt.
Germany's broad money supply
Australia's current-account deficit
Hungary's deficit
Korea's industrial production

Hinweis. Im Prinzip kann statt z.B. *America's output ...* auch stehen *output in America* oder *In America, output ...* Die Konstruktion mit *'s* wird bevorzugt, wenn in der Umgebung bereits eine Phrase mit *in* plus Substantiv steht.
The 12-month rate of growth in America's broad money supply, M3.

Dies gilt besonders dann, wenn zeitliche Angaben mit *in* gemacht werden.
America's visible-trade deficit rose sharply in October, to $15 billion.
Japan's consumer-price inflation quickened to 0.7% in October. beschleunigte sich ...
In October, America's 12-month broad-money growth fell to 1.3%.

Das *in* steht auch dann, wenn sich mit der *'s*-Konstruktion ein überlanges Subjekt ergeben würde.
Long-term youth unemployment is less than 10% in America, Canada, Japan and Sweden. [statt: *America's, Canada's, Japan's, Sweden's long-term youth unemployment ...*]
Unemployment rates fell slightly in America and Canada in October, to 5.8% and 10.0% respectively. ... auf 5,8% bzw. 10,0%.

In den letzten beiden Sätzen liegt außerdem der Nachdruck auf *America* usw., auch von daher wird die *'s*-Konstruktion vermieden.

Währungen. Verschiedene Aspekte, die Währungen betreffen, werden mit *'s* konstruiert.
the peso's exchange rate
the yen's rise
the D-mark's share

Auslassung nach 's. Die Ergänzung nach *'s* kann weggelassen werden, wenn sie aus dem Zusammenhang rekonstruierbar ist.
West German industry has since 1983 been the fastest of the four, overtaking Italy's [industry]. ... die in Italien
In the 12 months to August, France's industrial output grew by 5.2% and Italy's by 12.3%. ... das von Italien

Nationalitätsadjektive. Nationalitätsadjektive wie *American, German* usw. plus Substantiv konkurrieren ebenfalls mit der Konstruktion *America's, Germany's* usw. plus Substantiv.
In einigen Fällen ist die Wahl zwischen beiden Konstruktionen beliebig.
German retail sales fell by 2.2% in October.
Germany's retail sales fell by 2.9% in the twelve months to August.

Bei Ausdrücken, die zur engeren Terminologie gehören, findet sich die Konstruktion mit Nationalitätsadjektiv nur sehr selten, wenn der Ausdruck ein weiteres Adjektiv enthält (wie *annual, foreign* in den folgenden Beispielen).
America's annual growth rate
Germany's foreign assets
Im Zusammenhang mit *currency* wird das Nationalitätenadjektiv verwendet.
The American currency is expected to rise.
Gleichfalls mit dem Adjektiv gehen *firms, workers, wages.*

SHOULD – OUGHT TO

should. Mit *should* drückt man ein ‚sollte' aus. D.h., man äußert eine Meinung oder einen Rat: Etwas soll (irgendwie) gemacht werden. Oder man weist darauf hin, dass etwas entsprechend den Vorschriften bzw. unter den entsprechenden Umständen gemacht werden sollte.
Central bankers now know (or should know) all about reputation and credibility.
Earlier increases in interest rates in America and Britain should be cheered, not feared.
That temptation, though understandable, should be resisted.
There should be no doubt about what is at stake in today's negotiations. ... was auf dem Spiel steht ...
This second price is the one that should be used to calculate the change in living standards.
How should governments tackle tax cheats? ... mit Steuerbetrügern umgehen ...

Bei einem vorangehenden *if*-Satz im Präsens bedeutet *should* ‚müsste/sollte eigentlich (ist aber doch nicht unbedingt der Fall)'.
If consumption goes up or health services improve, fewer babies should die.
If the economy works efficiently, new job creation should offset job losses.

should steht in *that*-Sätzen nach Verben, Substantiven und Adjektiven. Der *that*-Satz bezieht sich auf ein zukünftiges Ereignis. Die vorangehenden Verben usw. beziehen sich auf Sagen, Beraten, Voraussagen, Argumentieren u.ä.
It may seem intuitively appealing that rich countries should give money to poorer ones to help them grow faster and live better.
Yet economic theory appeared to predict that the American version should be the most efficient.

The World Bank says that the power of the market should be harnessed to provide better infrastructure in developing countries. ... sollte ausgenützt werden ...
In 1949 the boss of IBM said the firm should have nothing to do with computers, because world demand could be satisfied by 10 or 15 machines.
They argue that all the non-German countries should devalue against the D-mark to boost their flagging economies. ... nachgebenden Wirtschaften ...

Mit *should have* und Partizip Perfekt wird formuliert, dass etwas hätte geschehen sollen (weil es so gut gewesen wäre, weil man selbst es so gewollt hätte), aber nicht geschehen ist.
The Bundesbank should have started easing policy much sooner. ... hätte viel früher beginnen sollen, eine nachgiebigere Politik zu verfolgen.

shall wird in Wirtschaftstexten kaum verwendet.

ought to. Damit wird formuliert, dass es gut/sinnvoll/wichtig ist, dass etwas geschieht.
Japan's use of industrial policy sets an example that America ought to follow.
... dem Amerika eigentlich nacheifern sollte.

ought to bedeutet, dass man Grund hat, etwas zu erwarten.
[This] ought to increase the value of households' consumption.

ought to bedeutet, dass etwas eigentlich eintreten müsste, doch ist man nicht ganz sicher.
In principle, you might think, consumers ought to gain partly at the expense of profits.

STEIGEN, MEHR WERDEN; FALLEN, WENIGER WERDEN; GLEICHBLEIBEN

Wirtschaftliche Entwicklungen werden bevorzugt mit Hilfe von Zahlen beschrieben, zeigen ein „Höher" oder „Mehr", ein „Tiefer" oder „Weniger", oder ein „Gleichbleiben". Für solche quantitativen Angaben steht ein bestimmtes Vokabular zur Verfügung, werden bestimmte Phrasen verwendet.

Die entsprechenden Teilabschnitte sind die Folgenden:
1. Mehr werden
2. Gleich bleiben
3. Weniger werden

Manche Vorgänge geschehen schneller, manche langsamer. Die entsprechenden Teilabschnitte sind:
4. Schneller
5. Langsamer

Siehe auch den Abschnitt VERGLEICH, ÄHNLICHKEIT, UNTERSCHIED.

In den einzelnen Einträgen werden die wichtigsten Substantive (wie etwa *growth, drop, fall, jump*) dargestellt, die Verben (z.B. *edge up, grow, fall, go up*), die Ergänzungen wie *by 6%, by 6% to 10%*, ferner, welche der Verben bevorzugt welche Subjekte oder Ergänzungen haben.

Hinweis: Verben und Ergänzungen
In den einzelnen Einträgen werden die Konstruktionsmöglichkeiten der Verben ausführlich dargestellt. Es lassen sich aber einige allgemeine Aussagen machen.
In der Regel werden die Verben nicht alleine verwendet, wie etwa in *Prices jumped in Norway* – aus dem einfachen Grund, dass in dieser Art von Bericht genauere Informationen erwartet werden. Ebenfalls dürftig ist eine Information wie *Output rose slightly,* entsprechend selten ist die Konstruktion Verb + Adverb. Die Kombination von Adverb und Zahlenangaben ist selten: *Prices rose slightly by 0.5%* ist eine Aussage, bei der entweder das *slightly* oder das *by 0.5%* wichtig ist, selten aber beides.
Die Regelangaben sind

Verb + Zahl ‚um'
Retail sales jumped 6.1% in the year to November.

Verb + *by* + Zahl (+ to + Zahl) ‚um (auf)'
Austria's producer prices rose by 2.7% [to 4%].

Verb + *to* + Zahl ‚auf'
Holland's current-account surplus increased to $8.4 billion.

Verb + *from* + Zahl + *to* + Zahl ‚von - bis, auf'
Sales of pirate cassettes declined slightly, from 680m to 675m.

1. Mehr werden

appreciate. *appreciate* ist ein Anziehen, vor allem von Währungen.
The South Korean won has fallen recently because of inflationary fears, having appreciated sharply between 1989 and 1992.
Note, however, the huge range of the forecasts for the rouble. The cheeriest seer expects it to appreciate by 27%, the gloomiest is forecasting a 26% drop.

climb. *climb* bezeichnet ein relativ starkes Steigen.
Istanbul was this week's star, climbing 10%.
Milan led the way, climbing by 3.6%.
In Britain, the annual broad-money growth rate climbed to 4.5% in November, from 3.8% in October.
Meanwhile, the D-mark's share rose to 19.7%; the yen's climbed to 8.7%.
Sugar supplies are tightening worldwide and prices have climbed above 13 cents a pound.

creep up, crept up, crept up. *creep up* bezeichnet ein etwas langsames, gegebenenfalls mühevolles Steigen.
In the 12 months to October consumer-price inflation crept up in the three East European economies in the table: from 10.5% to 10.7% in the Czech Republic ...
America's industrial output crept up by 0.7% in August.

edge up. Mit *edge up* wird eine geringe Zunahme oder Erhöhung bezeichnet.
In the same month, inflation edged up in both Mexico and Argentina.
... its producer-price inflation edged up to 2.4%.

Es wird häufig mit Subjekten wie Börsenorten, *inflation, production, rate, wages* verwendet.
Wall Street edged up by 0,2%.

expand. *expand* bezeichnet ein Vergrößern, Expandieren besonders, wenn eine Art Volumen vorliegt.
Malaysia's GDP expanded by 8.9% in the year to the third quarter.
... while continental Europe and Japan are forecast to expand more briskly.
expanding equity markets

go up, went up, gone up. Das Erhöhen kann mit *go up* formuliert werden (ist jedoch relativ selten).
... it went up to 2.6% in Britain.
In industrialised economies they went up by only 4%.

grow, grew, grown. Mit *grow* wird ein Wachsen bezeichnet.
Britain's industrial output grew by 6.7% in the 12 months to September.
Broad money grew by 4.0%, and narrow money by 5.3%.

Die häufigsten Subjekte sind *broad money, output, production, sales, money supply*.
Das Verb wird nur selten in Kontexten verwendet, die ein *present perfect (has/have grown)* erfordern.

growth. *growth* ist Wachstum. Es ist ein Singularwort und wird meist ohne den unbestimmten Artikel *a* verwendet.
Growth is expected to slow in both economies.

Die Angabe, dass ein Wachstum vorliegt, ist relativ unspezifiziert, daher kommt *growth* alleine nur selten vor.

Der Bereich, der wächst, kann durch Substantive oder Adjektive vor *growth* benannt werden.
Canada's annual GDP growth
annual broad-money growth
money-supply growth
real GNP growth
economic growth

Vor *growth* können auch Angaben zur Art oder Dauer stehen.
nervous about Australia's rapid growth
the 12-month growth in Holland's broad-money supply ...

‚Wachstums-' wird durch vorgestelltes *growth* ausgedrückt.
growth predictions
growth prospects
growth rate
broad-money growth rate

Der (seltene) Anschluss von Zahlen geschieht durch *of*.
real GNP growth of 3% or more

Der Bereich, für den ein Wachstum vorausgesagt wird, wird mit *in* angeschlossen.
the sluggish growth in real money in Britain and America
Israel's 12-month growth in industrial output
‚Wachstumsrate' ist *growth rate* oder *rate of growth*.

increase Verb. *increase* [ɪn'kriːs] ist ‚(sich) erhöhen'. Das Verb kann für sich alleine gebraucht werden.
Private-sector employment has increased.

Die Ergänzung mit *by* drückt das ‚um' aus.
In July Austria's broad-money measure increased by 5.4%.
Britain's retail sales increased by 3.3% in the 12 months to October.

Statt Zahlen können Angaben wie *sharply, most sharply, faster, rapidly* stehen.
China's sugar consumption is increasing rapidly.

Der Endpunkt der Erhöhung wird mit *to* angefügt.
Holland's current-account surplus increased to $8.4 billion.

Das Partizip der Vergangenheit kann als Adjektiv verwendet werden.
the increased sales

Increasingly ist ‚in zunehmendem Maß'.

increase Substantiv. *an increase* ['ɪnkriːs] ist eine Erhöhung. Das Substantiv kann alleine verwendet werden:
In Chile the increase was 11%.

Gängige Fügungen sind
rate of increase
pay increase
wage increase.

Die quantitative Angabe kann vorgestellt werden.
a 3.1% pay increase

Oder durch *of* angefügt werden.
an increase of 5%
Singapore and Istanbul also managed increases of 3% or more.

‚Erhöhung im Bereich von' ist *increase in:*
Recent years have seen a rapid increase in equity flows.
in the wake of an increase in the discount rate. im Gefolge ...

jump. *jump* ist eine (positive oder negative) schnelle Entwicklung nach oben.
Retail sales jumped 6.1% in the year to November. ... um ...
Japan's inflation jumped to 4.2% in the year to November. ... auf ...
Australia's industrial output jumped by 10.0% in the year to the third quarter.
... um ...

leap, leapt, leapt. *leap* ist ein starkes und schnelles Steigen.
Japanese retail sales leapt 7.5% in the 12 months to September.
In the same period, British industrial output leapt by 5.6%.

leap Substantiv. *a leap* ist ein schnelles und starkes Steigen.
The biggest leap was last year when $61 billion of net equity capital flowed into emerging stockmarkets, almost 20 times more than in 1986.

pick up. *pick up* ist ‚wieder auf dem Weg nach oben sein, sich erholen'.
Since 1990, however, investment has picked up.

raise. *raise* bezeichnet ein Anheben, meist das Anheben von Zinsen durch Banken.
The European markets lagged behind, as the Bundesbank raised its interest rates.
Canadian banks raised their prime lending rates by half a percentage point to 8.0%.
It raised interest rates a percentage point to 7.5%.
Its inflation forecast for 1995 has also been raised from 3.5% to 3.9%.
On December 20th Mexico's leaders agreed to raise by 0.53 pesos the upper limit of the peso's exchange-rate band against the dollar.

Im letzten Beispiel steht das *by 0.53 pesos* vor dem Objekt. Diese Stellung ist durch die Länge des Objekts (*the upper limit – dollar*) begründet.

rally. Das Verb *rally* ist ‚sich erholen'.
... the markets rallied a little when the German Lombard rate was increased ...

a rally ist eine Erholung (des Marktes).
after a brisk technical rally nach einer schnellen technischen Erholung

recover. *recover* ist ‚(sich) erholen'.
This year consumption is forecast to recover to 100,000 tonnes.
Sao Paulo recovered a little from lows.

recovery. Bei wirtschaftlichen Bereichen oder bei Börsen kann man von einer *recovery,* einer ‚Erholung', sprechen.
Japan's recovery is at last under way.

rise, rose, risen Verb. *rise* ist ‚mehr, höher werden, steigen'. Das Verb kann für sich alleine gebraucht werden.
Only one, Tokyo, rose: it gained 0,5%.
rise wird mit verschiedenen Ergänzungen gebraucht.
Switzerland's wholesale prices rose 0.7% in the 12 months to November. um
Copper rose above $2,700 a tonne. auf über
All of the top currencies rose against the dollar over the past year. gegenüber dem Dollar
Austria's producer prices rose by 2.7%.
Australia's retail sales rose by 2.8% in the year to the second quarter.
Venezuela's monthly inflation rose slightly to 5.1% in October.
Australia's broad money-supply growth rose to 8.5% in the year to October. auf
South Africa's financial rand rose to just under four rand to the dollar.

rise Substantiv. *a rise* ist eine Anhebung, insbesondere von Löhnen und Gehältern, Preisen, Zinsen. Zahlenangaben werden vorgestellt oder mit *of* eingeführt. Nach *rise* wird das, was erhöht wird, mit *in* angeschlossen.
a rise of only 0.6%
Japanese workers received a pay rise of 1.3%.
Italian employees got a 7.1% rise.
a sharp rise in interest rates
a rise in American interest rates

soar. *soar* bezeichnet ein schnelles Steigen, oft zusammen mit *industrial output*.
Although interest rates around the world have soared this year ...
Taiwan's industrial production soared by 12.9% in the 12 months to November.
Russian sales [of gold] are forecast to soar by 20% to 2.9m ounces.

widen. *widen* ‚sich vergrößern' wird mit Adverbien wie *slightly* verwendet oder mit Zahlenangaben oder mit beiden Typen von Angaben:
Spain's visible-trade deficit widened slightly in the year to September.
Canada's visible-trade surplus widened to $1.3 billion in October.
Brazil's 12-month visible-trade surplus widened slightly to $13.9 billion.

widen wird zusammen mit den Subjekten *deficit, surplus* verwendet. Siehe im Gegensatz dazu auch *narrow* in STEIGEN, MEHR WERDEN ..., dort in „3. Weniger werden".

2. Gleich bleiben

continue. *continue* drückt aus, dass ein bestimmter Vorgang sich fortsetzt. Es kann mit einem *to*-Infinitiv ergänzt werden.
Assuming cutbacks continue Angenommen ...
Borrowing on the international capital markets has continued to rise.
Imports, though, continued to increase.

continued ist ‚fortgesetzt':
continued economic gloom

continuing ist ‚andauernd':
continuing fears
continuing weakness

persist. *persist* ist ‚andauern'.
Warsaw's slump persisted.

persistent und *persistently:*
thanks to its persistent current-account deficits
persistently high levels of inflation

remain. *remain* ist ‚in der angegebenen Art/Position bleiben'. Zahlen werden mit *at* (= bei) angeschlossen.
In November western Germany's unemployment rate remained at 8.2% of the labour force.
Gängige Adjektive sind *(remain) high, low, buoyant, unchanged, positive.*

stay. *stay* ist ‚weiterhin sein, bleiben, verbleiben'. Zahlen werden mit *at* (= bei) angeschlossen.
Asia is expected to stay the star attraction.
Its share of developing countries' reserves has stayed more or less flat since 1980.
... ist praktisch gleichbleibend ...
Producer-price inflation stayed at 2.3%.

3. Weniger werden

decline Substantiv. *a decline* ist eine Abwärtsbewegung.
a decline of 0.1%
However, many emerging equity markets have performed poorly this year. Turkey's and China's have seen the biggest declines.
But its share of industrialised countries' reserves is in decline.

decline Verb. *decline* beschreibt eine Bewegung nach unten.
Only one country is expected to see its GNP decline between the two years: Sweden, with a 0.5% drop.
In the same period Britain's visible-trade deficit declined slightly to $30.8 billion.
In the year to the third quarter Australia's GDP declined by 1.9%. ... um ...
Sales of pirate cassettes declined slightly, from 680m to 675m.

drop Substantiv. *drop* beschreibt ein Sinken oder Fallen auf ein Niveau, das als unter Durchschnitt angesehen wird. Das Substantiv wird daher oft entsprechend modifiziert.
the biggest daily drop for nine months
despite a massive drop in output in Russia

Die Erweiterung durch Zahlen:
a 20.4% drop; a 26% drop

Der Bereich, in dem sich das Abwärts ereignet, wird mit *in* formuliert.
a 20.4% drop in production
a massive drop in output

drop Verb. In der Regel werden Orts- und/oder Zeitangaben zugefügt.
Both Frankfurt and Milan dropped by more than 3%.
Denmark's jobless rate dropped to 12.2% in August.
The countries' reserves held in dollars dropped from 87% to 60.7%.
Annual broad-money growth also dropped in Germany, to 7.4%.

Die Intensivierung des Verbs geschieht durch *sharply*.
Germany's trade surplus dropped sharply in July.

Verb und Substantiv *drop* werden in formeller Berichterstattung seltener verwendet.

edge down. Mit *edge down* wird ein nur geringes Fallen oder Verringern bezeichnet.
In the same month Germany's jobless rate edged down to 6.2%.

fall Substantiv. *a fall* ist eine Verringerung. Das Wort kann für sich stehen.
Sweden and Switzerland also show falls.

Es ist modifizierbar, wie in
a 3.8% fall
a modest fall
a substantial fall.

Zahlenangaben werden auch mit *of* angeschlossen. Solche Angaben sind jedoch seltener.
a fall of 32%

Der Bereich, für den der *fall* gilt, wird mit *in* angeschlossen.
the fall in Brazil's output
the fall in net coal exports

Die Verringerung ‚gegenüber' ist *fall against*.
a 86% fall in its currency against the dollar
a modest fall against the dollar

fall, fell, fallen. Das Verb wird nur selten alleine verwendet.
Russian exports are expected to fall.
Output of mined lead has also fallen.

Die Zahl unmittelbar nach *fall* ist als ‚um ...' zu verstehen. Die Konstruktion ist selten.
Canada's industrial output fell 2.8%.
The surplus is expected to fall around 100,000 tonnes.

Das Fallen gegenüber einem bestimmten Maßstab ist *fall against.*
In the next three months, all but one of the 22 currencies in our table is expected to fall against the dollar.

fall back ist ‚zurückfallen'.
The Shanghai stockmarket then fell back after a denial by the government.

fall below ist das Fallen unter einen bestimmten Wert.
London Metal Exchange stocks have fallen below 2m tonnes from a peak of 2.7m.

fall by ist das Fallen um einen bestimmten Wert. Es ist die Konstruktion, die am häufigsten auftritt.
Malaysian tin output is expected to fall by 18% in 1995.
... and production is expected to fall by a fifth this year.
The Brazilian real is forecast to fall by 14% over the next six months.

Die Konstruktion kann durch *from* erweitert werden.
Western mine supply has already fallen by 35% from its peak in 1980.

Mit *fall from* + Zahl + *to* + Zahl wird die Größe der Verringerung durch zwei Werte zu verschiedener Zeit angegeben.
[This] helped British inflation to fall from 7.7% to 5.8%.

In vielen Fällen steht eine Ortsangabe oder eine Angabe der Zeit.
America's retail sales fell in July.
Government bond yields fell in Europe.

Das Ausmaß der Verringerung kann – ohne Zahl – durch Adverbien wie (meist) *slightly* ‚gering', *sharply* ‚stark' angegeben werden.
Unemployment rates fell slightly in America and Canada.
Employment has fallen sharply in all East European economies.
Australia's rate has fallen most sharply. ... am stärksten ...

fall to ist das Zurückgehen auf einen bestimmten, genannten Wert.
Australia's jobless rate fell to 11.3% in December.

narrow Verb. *narrow* bezeichnet ein Wenigerwerden, Sich-Verringern. Es wird vor allem zusammen mit den Subjekten *surplus* und *deficit* gebraucht.
Germany's visible-trade surplus narrowed to $24.5 billion.
Japan's current-account surplus narrowed slightly to $130.4 billion ...
Japan's visible-trade surplus narrowed slightly, to $145.2 billion.
Poland's trade deficit narrowed slightly, to $800m.

plummet. *plummet* bezeichnet eine rapide Bewegung nach unten, ein Stürzen.
Share prices plummeted in Warsaw and Prague this week.
Our seers expect the Hungarian forint to plummet by 13.7% from its current rate.

plunge Substantiv. *a plunge* ist ein starkes und schnelles Fallen, Abstürzen.
a 32% plunge over the past three months
... following an even bigger plunge ...
They also predict a plunge in the value of the Russian rouble.

plunge Verb. *plunge* bezeichnet ein starkes und schnelles Fallen, ein Abstürzen.
French industrial output plunged 4.5% in November.
Share prices in Mexico City plunged by 9.6% this week.
Coffee prices plunged this week to their lowest level.

shrink, shrank, shrunk. *shrink* beschreibt eine Abnahme, es wird zusammen mit Subjekten gebraucht, die ein „Volumen" haben, wie *deficit, surplus, supply*.
Its current-account deficit shrank to $27.2 billion.
Its 12-month deficit has shrunk to $20.5 billion.
the sluggish growth in real money in Britain and America (where the real-money supply has actually been shrinking) ...
a shrinking surplus

slump Verb. *slump* bezeichnet ein starkes Zurückgehen, einen Verfall von Preisen bzw. wirtschaftlichen Aktivitäten.
Russia's domestic demand has slumped.
Tokyo slumped by 2.4%.
Russia's GDP slumped by 16%.

slump Substantiv. *slump* bezeichnet ein starkes Zurückgehen, einen Verfall von Preisen bzw. wirtschaftlichen Aktivitäten.
the slump in the building and car industries
a marked slump in imports

4. Schneller

quicken Verb. *quicken* ist ‚sich beschleunigen'. Der erreichte Wert wird mit *to* angefügt. Angaben mit *by*, die erläutern, um wie viel sich ein Wert verändert hat, sind selten. Angaben wie *slightly* können hinzutreten. Die häufigsten Subjekte zu *quicken* sind *growth, inflation, rate*.
Australia's inflation rate quickened slightly to 1.9% in the year.
America's GDP growth quickened to 4.3% in the year to the third quarter.

fast. *fast (faster, fastest)* wird als Adjektiv und Adverb verwendet, ‚schnell'. Das gemeinsprachliche *quick(ly)* ist sehr selten.
the fastest rate since 1981
Japan is predicted to be the OECD's fastest grower in 1991.
significantly faster growth
West German industry has since 1983 been the fastest of the four, overtaking Italy's.
fast-growing economies
The output of Japan's industry has grown faster than that of any other of the seven largest OECD members.
Prices rose fastest last year in South Africa, by 10.9%.

speedy. *speedy* ist ‚schnell, beschleunigt'.
The speedy growth of the four countries ...

5. Langsamer

slow Verb. *slow* ist ‚im Aufstieg/Abstieg langsamer werden'.
In October, Belgium's inflation rate slowed to 2.1%.
Italy's 12-month rate of broad-money growth slowed from 6.6% in July to 5.4% in August.

Its narrow-money growth rate also slowed, to 6.5%.
The Czech Republic's growth rate slowed sharply, to 1.2% ...
Britain's GDP growth slowed slightly to 3.6% ...

slow(ly) Adjektiv (Adverb). *slow* ist ‚langsam'.
Latin American exports have also been growing more slowly than Asia's.
Someone is slow to do something bedeutet, dass jemand lange braucht, um etwas zu tun.
The dispersion of a new technology is not just slow but extraordinarily uncertain.
Why have governments been so slow to make use of their new freedom to cut interest rates?

STEUER

revenue. *revenue* ['revənjuː] bezeichnet die Einnahmen des Staates durch Steuern *(tax revenue)*.
The economic slowdown erodes tax revenue.
countries where tax revenues are small
revenue authorities Steuerbehörde
revenue tariff Finanzzoll

fiscal. Das Adjektiv *fiscal* ist ‚öffentliche Gelder, Steuern, Ausgaben betreffend'.
fiscal policy ist die Finanzpolitik eines Staates. Je nach folgendem Substantiv ist es ‚Steuer-' oder ‚Finanz-'.
fiscal measures steuerliche Maßnahmen
fiscal crises Finanzkrisen
fiscal jurisdiction Steuerhoheit

tax Verb. *tax* (ohne Objekt) ist ‚Steuern einrichten', mit Objekt ‚besteuern'.
Governments have the power to tax.
a way of taxing company profits
the most heavily taxed fuel
If people do not feel heavily taxed ...
gas, which is usually taxed lightly, ...

What is the best way to tax multinational companies?
taxing all fuels at more similar rates

tax Substantiv. Die Erhebung von Steuern auf etwas: *a tax/taxes on something.*
taxes on coal, gas and oil
taxes on video recorders
taxes on income

after/before tax ist ‚nach/vor Steuerabzug'.

Das Besteuerte kann auch als Substantiv vor *tax/taxes* stehen.
capital gains tax Steuer auf Vermögensgewinne
carbon tax Steuer auf Kohlendioxyd-Verbrauch
cigarette taxes
consumption tax Verbrauchsteuer
energy tax
export tax
fuel taxes
income tax Einkommensteuer
oil tax
petrol tax

Mit vorangestellten Adjektiven:
corporate tax Körperschaftsteuer
direct tax direkte (nicht abwälzbare) Steuer
indirect tax
flat tax vereinheitlichte Steuer
value-added tax (VAT) Mehrwertsteuer

Mit *tax* als erstem Element:
tax allowance Steuerfreibetrag
tax base Besteuerungsgrundlage
tax-free steuerfrei
tax authorities Steuerbehörden
tax avoidance Steuerumgehung
tax benefit Steuervergünstigung
tax bill Steuergesetz, auch: Steuerbescheid
tax break Steuervergünstigung
tax burden Steuerlast, steuerliche Belastung
tax cheat Steuerbetrüger
tax credit Steuergutschrift

tax cut Steuersenkung
tax declaration Steuererklärung
tax-deductible steuerlich abzugsfähig
tax dodger jemand, der (legal) Steuern vermeidet
tax evasion Steuerhinterziehung
tax increase
tax privilege Steuervergünstigung
tax rate Steuersatz
tax reform
tax revenue Steueraufkommen des Staates
tax system

Verben mit *tax* als Objekt: *pay* (abführen), *abolish* (abschaffen), *impose on someone* (auferlegen, einführen), *raise* (erheben), *levy* (einziehen, erheben), *increase* (erhöhen), *remit* (erlassen, nicht zahlen müssen), *assess* (festsetzen), *evade* (hinterziehen), *cut* (senken).

taxable. Was zu versteuern/steuerpflichtig ist, ist *taxable*.
taxable income steuerpflichtiges Einkommen
taxable profits steuerpflichtiger Gewinn
to be taxable as ordinary income als normales Einkommen versteuerbar

taxation. *taxation* ist ‚das Besteuern, die Besteuerung'
the taxation of different goods and services

taxman. *the taxman* wird als Personifikation der Steuerbehörden verwendet, in etwa ‚der Fiskus'.

taxpayer. *taxpayer* ist jeder, der Steuern zahlen muss bzw. zahlt. Das Wort wird aber nicht, wie im Deutschen gelegentlich, im Sinne von „wir, die kleinen Steuerzahler" verwendet.

SUBSTANTIVE

Im Englischen unterscheidet man zwischen verschiedenen Arten von Substantiven. Die wichtigste Unterscheidung ist die zwischen Substantiven, die eine Singular- und eine Pluralform haben (wie *table – tables, book – books*) und Substantiven, die nur die Singularform haben, wie z.B. *information, employment*. Im ersten Falle *(table – tables)* spricht man von *count nouns*, im zweiten Falle *(information)* von *non-count nouns* oder *uncount nouns*.

Ein *count noun* kann u.a. zusammen mit den Artikeln *a/an* oder *the* stehen, auch mit Zahlwörtern: *a table, the table, two tables*. Dagegen nicht: **an information, *two informations*.

If unemployment starts to rise ... Wenn sich die Arbeitslosigkeit erhöht ...
an effort to combat inflation eine Anstrengung, die Inflation zu bekämpfen
the costs of research and development
Under pessimistic assumptions, damage could be nearly 20% of world GDP
... könnte der Schaden/könnten die Schäden ...

Will man sich dennoch, bei Verwendung von *non-count nouns*, ausdrücklich auf ein einzelnes oder auf mehrere einzelne Vorkommnisse beziehen, muss man umschreibend konstruieren, z.B. *a piece of information, a piece of advice, a period of inflation*.

Unter gewissen Umständen kann vor einem *non-count noun* der bestimmte Artikel stehen: meist dann, wenn ein Relativsatz oder eine ähnliche Konstruktion folgt oder wenn zum zweiten Male vom Gleichen die Rede ist.
the damage done by dams der Schaden, der durch Staudämme entsteht
the damage that might be prevented der Schaden, der verhindert werden könnte
... *the damage would be slight*.

Es empfiehlt sich, im Zweifelsfalle die Lernerwörterbücher des Englischen zu konsultieren.

Es gibt Substantive, die sowohl *count nouns* als auch *non-count nouns* sind, wie etwa *return* ‚Ertrag', *tax* ‚Steuer'. Es gibt auch solche, die in einer Bedeutung *non-count* sind (*economy* ‚Sparsamkeit') und in einer anderen *count nouns* (*economy/economies* ‚Wirtschaftssystem/e'). *investment* ist ‚das Investieren', *an investment* ist u.a. eine investierte Summe.

Substantive, die Fachrichtungen bezeichnen, z.B. *economics, statistics, mathematics* ‚die Mathematik', *physics* ‚die Physik' werden im Singular konstruiert.

Manche Substantive werden nur im Plural konstruiert und haben keine Singularform: *goods* ‚Waren', *damages* ‚Schadenersatz'.

Kombinationen:
Sehr viele der Substantive können als erstes oder zweites Element in Kombinationen verwendet werden.
export growth
money market
price stability
tax reduction
consumer price
capital gain
income tax

Das erste Element hat fast immer die Singularform. Bei diesen Kombinationen ist zu beachten, dass in manchen Fällen das zweite Element betont wird *(capital GAINS)*, manchmal kann sowohl auf dem ersten Element oder auf dem zweiten Element betont werden *(merchant BANK – MERchant bank, MOney market – money MARket)*. Die Regeln für die eine oder andere Betonung sind kompliziert und nicht gut bekannt. Wenn man Wirtschaftsberichte hört, empfiehlt es sich, auf die verwendete Betonung zu achten.

Wenn mehr als zwei Substantive kombiniert werden, wird häufig ein Bindestrich zwischen die beiden gesetzt, die enger zusammen gehören.
consumer-price stability
money-market assistance
income tax-credit

Manche Substantive gehen nur selten Verbindungen mit anderen ein. Eine Wirtschaftstheorie ist keine **economy theory* sondern eine *economic theory,* ebenso *financial measures, environmental policy, monetary policy.*

TERMINOLOGIE

Die Fachbegriffe der Wirtschaftssprache bergen einige Schwierigkeiten. Zum einen mag das daran liegen, dass man die Bedeutung bestimmter Wörter anfangs nicht kennt, wie *bearish* ‚auf Baisse gerichtet (Börse)' oder *sluggish* ‚lustlos (Börse)'. Zum andern erscheinen manche Fachbegriffe lang und kompliziert, wie *capital markets external surpluses.*

Die wesentlichen Komplikationen haben jedoch einen anderen Grund. Die „Wirtschaft" ist weder ein kleiner noch ein sorgfältig abgegrenzter Bereich. Wirtschaftliche Texte handeln von Hochtechnologie, von Konjunkturlagen, vom Börsengeschehen, vom Handels- und Vertragsrecht, von Banken, Arbeitslosigkeit, Umweltproblemen, von Werbung, Verkauf, Export und vielen weiteren Bereichen. (Wirtschaftstexte handeln auch von Ereignissen und Zuständen, die die Wirtschaft betreffen: von Wahlen, Umstürzen, Kriegen, Naturkatastrophen, politischen Systemen, Bildungssystemen u.a.)

Man kann daher nicht erwarten, dass ein bestimmtes Wort, ein bestimmter Ausdruck immer nur in derselben Bedeutung verwendet wird. Schlägt man in einem Wirtschaftswörterbuch unter *interest* nach, so findet sich eine größere Zahl möglicher Übersetzungen: „Vorteil, Interesse, Belange, Nutzen, Bedeutung, Interesse, Wichtigkeit, Zinsen, Zinsfuß, Verzinsung, Anrecht, Anspruch, Versicherungsinteresse, Beteiligung, Anteil".

Diese Vielfalt von prinzipiellen Übersetzungen erklärt sich zum einen daraus, dass wirtschaftliche Texte auch die Gemeinsprache verwenden (*interest* als ‚Interesse'), zum andern daraus, dass in einzelnen Sparten manche Wörter in verschiedener Bedeutung eingesetzt werden (Bankwesen: ‚Zins, Zinsfuß'; Versicherungswesen: ‚Versicherungsinteresse'). In der Wirtschaftssprache wird mit vielen solcher allgemeinen Wörter operiert: *interest, gains, rate, capital, market, credit, book, proof, account, product* usw.

Diese Wörter sind keine Fachwörter im strengen Sinne; zu solchen werden sie erst in Kombination, z.B. *domestic, demand* → *domestic demand* ‚Inlandsnachfrage' (→ *domestic demand growth*) oder *capital, goods, sector* → *capital goods sector* ‚Investitionsgüterbereich'.

Bei den Kombinationen ist Folgendes zu beachten.

a) Manche der Kombinationen aus Substantiven können in Kombinationen umgeändert werden, die eine Präposition enthalten, etwa *growth rate* → *rate of growth; income taxes* → *taxes on income*. Die Wahl der einen oder anderen Kombination hängt von den Gegebenheiten des jeweiligen Satzes ab.

b) Substantivkombinationen im Deutschen müssen keine Entsprechung im Englischen haben. So gibt es kein **economy theory, *economy growth, *increase economy*. Solche „kombinationsunwilligen" Wörter erscheinen dann oft in der Form eines Adjektivs, also *economic theory* (‚Wirtschaftstheorie'), *economic growth* (‚Wirtschaftswachstum'), *financial measures* (und nicht **finance measures*).

c) Die Regeln, nach denen – in der Aussprache – Substantivkombinationen betont werden, sind ziemlich kompliziert und noch nicht recht klar: *GROWTH rate, MONey market, export BUsiness, capital exPENditure, MOney market asSIStance*. Man sollte, wenn man diese Wörter zum ersten Mal hört, auf deren Betonung achten.

UMWELT

carbon dioxide. *carbon dioxide* [kɑːbən 'daɪɒksaɪd] ist Kohlendioxyd CO2.
the output of carbon dioxide
carbon-dioxide output

Gelegentlich wird in derselben Bedeutung die verkürzte Form *carbon* verwendet. *growth in carbon-dioxide content* wird allgemein als Gefahr gesehen, daher ist der entsprechende *output* zu reduzieren *(reduce, curb)*. Ein ökonomisches Mittel hierfür ist die Einführung einer *carbon tax*.

damage. Siehe *damage* in GEFAHREN, PROBLEME, SCHWIERIGKEITEN.

environment. *environment* [ɪn'vaɪrənmənt] ‚Umwelt' wird mit dem bestimmten Artikel verwendet (weil es nur eine Umwelt gibt, so auch *the sun, the moon*). Im Sinne von ‚Umgebung', ‚lokale Umwelt' kann es auch im Plural stehen.
economic approaches to the environment
the value of the environment to future generations

Kombinationen von Substantiv plus *environment* oder *environment* plus Substantiv sind selten. ‚Umwelt-' oder ‚die Umwelt betreffend' wird durch das Adjektiv *environmental* ausgedrückt.
environmental conference
environmental damage Umweltschäden
environmental debate Umweltdiskussion

Häufige Kombinationen von *environmental* mit Substantiven sind: *decision, economists, effects, figures, groups, investment, law, loss, measures, policies, problems, programme, protection, quality, regulations, tax.*

Personen, die sich für den Umweltschutz engagieren, sind *environmentalists*, dazu das Adjektiv *environmentalist*.

fuels. *fuels* sind Brennstoffe, *fossil fuels* fossile Brennstoffe. Sie werden verbrannt *(burnt)*, sie sind mit Steuern belegt *(taxed)*: *carbon tax, fuel tax, energy tax.*
oil, at present the most heavily taxed fuel in OECD countries
petrol and diesel fuel
domestic heating fuel
jet fuel

Das Verb *fuel* kann ‚beleben, stärken' bedeuten.
They would fuel inflationary expectations.
to fuel recovery

Klima, Treibhaus, Erwärmung, Ausstoß. Ein Klimawechsel *(climate change, climatic change)* wird befürchtet. Er ist durch den Treibhauseffekt *(greenhouse effect)* bewirkt, durch die *greenhouse gases,* z.b. *carbon dioxide* oder *chlorofluorocarbons CFCs* (Fluorchlorkohlenwasserstoffe FCKWs), diese letzteren schädigen *(damage)* auch die Ozonschicht *(ozone layer).* Diese Gase sind *emissions.* Der Klimawechsel besteht im *global warming – an incalculable risk.*
The greenhouse effect will cause the earth's temperature to rise.
the impact of global warming
positive steps to curb global warming
a reduction of greenhouse gases by 10%
carbon dioxide, the main greenhouse gas
The consequences of climate change might be catastrophic.
stabilising emissions of carbon dioxide at 1990 levels

pollution. *pollution* ‚(Umwelt)Verschmutzung' wird nur im Singular gebraucht und ohne den unbestimmten Artikel *a.*
air pollution **Luftverschmutzung**
cross-border pollution **grenzübergreifende Verschmutzung**
global pollution
pollution prevention
pollution control

Das dazugehörige Verb ist *pollute.* Die Partizipien hierzu können als Adjektive verwendet werden.
a polluting country **Verschmutzung verursachend**
old polluting factories
a polluted river

Die Verursacher der Verschmutzung sind *polluters.*

URSACHEN, FOLGEN, BEGRÜNDUNGEN

after. Die Präposition und die Konjunktion sind in den meisten Fällen als zeitliches ‚nach' bzw. ‚nachdem' zu verstehen.
After last week's falls, all but three of the stock markets in our table rose this week. Nach den Verlusten der letzten Woche ...
Gelegentlich ist in dem Nacheinander eine Kausalität zumindest impliziert.
Share prices in Mexico City plunged by 9.6% this week after reports of renewed trouble in the state of Chiapas. ... im Gefolge von Berichten ...
American farmers are harvesting their biggest crop for almost 60 years, after high prices persuaded them to plant more.

as. Die Bedeutung der Konjunktion *as* ist in den meisten Fällen ‚da, weil'.
In recessions public spending tends to be pushed up as unemployment benefits increase ...
In fast-growing economies p/e ratios tend to be high, as share prices reflect expectations of much higher company earnings to come.
China's sugar consumption is increasing rapidly as incomes rise and people consume more soft drinks, alcohol and ice-cream.
Exporters also favour the move, as more of the current crop will be available for export.
Japan, which once had the cheapest short-term capital, rose to 11th, as its real interest rates more than doubled to 2.49%.
Wheat prices have climbed above $4 a bushel this month as supplies have tightened worldwide. ... da die Vorräte weltweit knapper geworden sind.

Gelegentlich bleibt offen, ob der mit *as* eingeführte Sachverhalt eine Begründung ist oder nur eine Begleiterscheinung, die möglicherweise kausal aufgefasst werden kann.
Milan fell by 1.6% as the government's budget problems continued.
Die Konjunktion *as* kann eine Gleichzeitigkeit ausdrücken.
That means ensuring that inflation remains low as recovery strengthens. Das bedeutet: Sicherstellen, dass die Inflation niedrig bleibt, während sich die Wirtschaft erholt.
As the recovery gathers pace, unemployment will fall.
The mine was closed last September when Brazil informally agreed with the Association of Tin Producers to limit its tin exports ...

base Verb. Ansichten, Darstellungen, Voraussagen, die ‚auf etwas beruhen' sind *based on something*.
The chart, based on an OECD study, shows income taxes ...

because. Die Konjunktion *because* leitet einen (adverbialen) Nebensatz ein, der eine Begründung formuliert, ‚da, weil'. Der Nebensatz steht in der Regel nach dem Hauptsatz.
Many economists argue that poor countries stay poor because they suffer from a shortage of capital.
If inflation stays low in this cycle, it will be because of better policy, not because the world is safer.
Many governments fear a high real exchange rate because it makes exports less competitive and imports cheaper ...
A strong euro can only benefit America because the existence of another important currency will compel it to greater discipline.

Das *because* selbst kann modifiziert werden:
perhaps because vielleicht weil
partly because teilweise weil
probably because wahrscheinlich weil
mainly because hauptsächlich weil
not least because nicht zuletzt deshalb, weil

Mit *that/this is because* wird ausgedrückt ‚dies ist der Fall, weil'.

because of. *because of* ist ‚wegen'.
because of mounting interest payments
because of the legal fees that have to be paid
because of shortages of jet fuel
partly because of the magnitude of the slump
This is mainly because of the huge gap between urban and rural incomes. Das ist im wesentlichen deshalb der Fall, weil ...

blame Verb. Mit *blame* wird eine Begründung gegeben und gleichzeitig eine Schuldzuweisung.
Who is to blame? Wer ist schuld daran?
... some of Europe's unemployment can be blamed on the recent recession ...
... kann ... angelastet werden ...

Miners blame the fall in world prices – down by almost half in 18 months, to $5,700 a tonne. ... sehen die Schuld bei ...
Product-market barriers may be as much to blame as labour-market rigidities for Western Europe's high rate of unemployment ... sind genau so verantwortlich für ...
Das Substantiv *blame* wird mit *for* konstruiert.
the blame for unemployment die Schuld an der Arbeitslosigkeit

cause Substantiv. *cause* ist ‚Grund, Ursache'. Mit anschließendem *of* wird der ‚Grund von' bezeichnet.
The real cause is structural.
the causes of high unemployment
the monetary causes of inflation

Wird *cause* mit *for* ergänzt, bedeutet es ‚Anlass':
little cause for concern wenig Anlass zur Sorge

cause Verb. *cause* bedeutet ‚der Grund für etwas sein, verursachen'.
Deregulation actually caused a big increase.
Since Saddam Hussein did not cause the recession, he cannot end it.

Die entsprechende Passivkonstruktion mit *by* wird häufig verwendet.
the falls in output caused by these factors
a surge in timber prices caused by a supply shortage in America

Mit einem Objekt und einem Infinitiv nach *to* ist *cause* ‚führen zu'.
... and that may cause demand to fall.
Deregulation ought to cause these profits to be competed away. ... dazu führen, dass diese Gewinne durch den Wettbewerb wieder verloren gehen.

caused to ist ‚(jemandem) entstanden':
the losses caused to investors

consequence. *a/the consequence* ‚Folge, Ergebnis, Konsequenz' hat in der Regel Ergänzungen mit *of* (‚von') bzw. *for* (‚für').
One consequence of these huge gains was that ...
the long-term consequences of current policies
serious consequences for the real economy

‚infolge, als Folge' kann mit *as a consequence* ausgedrückt werden.
If workers get less training as a consequence ...

Das Adjektiv *consequent* bedeutet ‚unmittelbar anschließend':
the consequent drop in demand

depend Verb. Die Abhängigkeit eines Vorgangs von anderen wird mit *depend on/ upon* ausgedrückt. Dies kann mit einer Substantivphrase konstruiert werden.
The natural [unemployment] rate depends upon things such as the generosity of unemployment benefits and labour mobility.

Oder mit einem Nebensatz, der mit *that, what, how, whether, when* usw. beginnt.
This partly depends on how additional environmental spending is financed.
... hängt teilweise davon ab, wie ...
Its participation in EMU will depend upon whether or not its deficit exceeds its investment.
Russia needs to be persuaded that the success of its own reforms will depend on keeping trade flowing among the republics.

dependence, dependent. *dependence* ist das Substantiv, *dependent* das Adjektiv zu *depend*.
... evidence of Asian dependence on Japan is hard to find.
... whether one country is financially dependent on another ...

independent (of) ist ‚unabhängig (von)'.

due to. *be due to* ist ‚liegt an, liegt/ist begründet in/ist zurückzuführen auf'. Dieses *due to* wird von einer Substantivphrase gefolgt.
Britain's net external balance has improved of late, in spite of current-account deficits. This has mainly been due to capital gains on its existing stock of foreign assets.
This is largely due to Brazil's so-far successful struggle to tame inflation.
The falls in output caused by these factors were not due to trade reform.

Häufig wird ein Nebensatz ohne Verb (das *due to X* in Kommas) verwendet.
An unsustainably high rate of credit growth, due to a sharp jump in the number of banks, forced the country's central bank to tighten up.

due to wird auch als Präposition konstruiert.
A temporary rise in unemployment due to recession ... ... Arbeitslosigkeit infolge einer Rezession

Weitere Ausführungen zu *due*, siehe *due* in ZEIT, dort in „2.3 Zukunft".

explain Verb. *explain* ist (kausal) erklären.
The speedy growth of the four countries ... only partly explains their big deficits.
Such differences are largely explained by funds' investment patterns.
This explains why the dollar has fallen by only 8% in trade-weighted terms over the past 12 months.

follow Verb. Mit *follow* kann eine Schlussfolgerung formuliert werden.
Investment is good for growth. A fall in the real rate of interest, it clearly follows, is just what any economy needs.
Although low inflation is rightly the prime objective of monetary policy, it does not follow that inflation makes the best operational target.

Viele Verwendungen von *follow* sind aber eher zeitlich (,nacheinander'), also nur in einem losen Sinne kausal.
And a sharp fall in lending followed ...
Following deregulation in the 1980s, British building societies can now raise money on the capital markets ... Nach/im Gefolge ...

Eine Argumentationsreihe kann so eingeführt werden:
The argument runs as follows.

for. *for fear that* und *for fear of* sind gleichbedeutend mit *on fear that* usw. Siehe *on* in diesem Abschnitt.

ground Substantiv, Verb. Das Substantiv *ground* kann im Sinne von ,Grund' verwendet werden (jedoch auch als ,Boden' wie in *lose ground, gain ground*). Es wird zusammen mit *on* ,aus' gebraucht.
on statistical grounds aus Gründen der Statistik
... where the feebleness of democratic institutions gives grounds for belief that living standards are suppressed by policy, not poverty. ... Grund für die Annahme gibt, dass ...

Their doubts are not mainly on the ground of budgetary costs ...
on the grounds that mit der Begründung, dass

Das Verb steht im Passiv zusammen mit *in*.
The case for deregulation can be grounded in empirical evidence.

hence. *hence* wird (als Adverb) im Sinne von ‚und daher, daher auch' verwendet, vor allem in kommentierenden Texten.
An upturn in inflation is due in Britain – and hence a rise in interest rates was overdue.
Hence the enthusiasm of some economists for a rule ...
That shifts resources to more efficient uses, which boosts productivity and hence living standards. ... was die Produktivität und daher auch den Lebensstandard kräftig erhöht.

imply. *imply* kann, ähnlich wie *mean,* als ‚führen zu, bedeuten' gebraucht werden.
So policies to cut gas output below the current level will imply a larger and larger reduction below projected levels as years go by.
It seems unlikely that an increase in the national average does not imply some improvement for the worst off.

lead, led, led Verb. *lead to* ist ‚führen zu'.
Indeed, Brazil's inflation led to an 86% fall in its currency against the dollar ...

Die Passivkonstruktion mit *led* bedeutet ‚angeführt, in die Wege geleitet'.
The recovery has been led by strong export growth, especially in manufacturing and timber.

mean, meant, meant. *mean* kann als ‚Folgen haben, führen zu' verwendet werden.
Dieses *mean* kann mit einem *that*-Satz erweitert werden.
Faster growth does not necessarily mean higher inflation. Schnelleres Wachstum muss nicht unbedingt zu höherer Inflation führen.
Unions predict that this will mean job and wage cuts in America.
Higher taxes also mean that workers have to work longer hours.

on. Die Präposition *on* wird im Sinne von ‚aufgrund/im Gefolge von' verwendet, zusammen mit Substantiven, die ‚Unruhe, Furcht, Sorge' ausdrücken, vor allem in Börsenberichten.
But Tokyo tumbled 7.6% on fears of a new political scandal.
Hong Kong fell 1.6% on worries about a rise in American interest rates.
Zu *on* in Verbindung mit *ground* siehe *ground* in diesem Abschnitt.

owing to. *owing to* wird in formellen Texten als Präposition verwendet: ‚wegen, infolge von'.
The ratio recovered fractionally in the first quarter of 1989, owing to a relative acceleration in prices in the northern regions.

reason Substantiv. *a/the reason* ist ‚Grund'. Das Wort wird in einer Reihe von Konstruktionen gebraucht. Hinweis: Die Konstruktion **the reason of* wird nicht verwendet.

Whatever the reasons was immer die Gründe (dafür) sein mögen
... for two reasons aus zwei Gründen
for another reason aus einem anderen Grund
for that reason aus diesem Grund

Der Grund für etwas wird mit *for* eingeführt.
There is no single reason for the divergence in real exchange rates between Latin America and Asia.
If there is any reason for thinking that in this cycle inflation may stay low ...

‚der Grund dafür, dass etwas der Fall ist' wird so konstruiert:
... the main reason for prices staying broadly stable ...

Mit *reason that* wird ‚der Grund, dass', ‚aus dem Grund, dass' formuliert.
Many oppose the shift to VAT for the very reason that it makes the tax system less progressive. ... aus genau dem Grund ...

Nach *reason* kann eine Infinitivkonstruktion mit *to* stehen.
That is one reason to expect that its rapid growth can continue.
There is no reason to fear that the Uruguay round discriminates against the poor.
There are good reasons to believe ...

Mit *reason why* wird ‚der Grund, warum', ‚der Grund, aus dem' konstruiert.
There are good reasons why official income indicators might underestimate the amount of money people have. Es gibt gute Gründe, warum ...

Dieses *why* kann ausgelassen werden.
The reason most prices have fallen in real terms is the price-capping formula ...

reason kann von einer Form von *be* und einem *that*-Satz gefolgt werden, der den Grund nennt.
The reason is that benefits are withdrawn as earnings rise.

Das Adjektiv *reasonable* ist ‚vernünftig, vernunftgemäß'.

reflect Verb. *reflect* bedeutet, dass sich eine Entwicklung in einer anderen zeigt, diese widerspiegelt (ein angedeuteter kausaler Zusammenhang).
Recent years have seen significant economic reforms, however, which are reflected in expanding equity markets.
In part that reflects the growth of trade between Japan and fast-growing East Asia.

reflect wird häufig als *reflecting*, wie im folgenden Satz, konstruiert.
In the year to the fourth quarter it [productivity growth] fell to 0.6%, reflecting the slowdown in output growth.

result Verb. *result from* wird als ‚resultieren von/aus' gebraucht, *result in* als ‚resultieren in'.
The increase in German demand resulting from unification ...
Such policies will result in a cut in the growth of global GDP.
The Bundesbank's fear of inflation and the impact of unification on Germany's budget deficit have resulted in higher real interest rates in Germany ...

Das Partizip kann als ‚resultierend, sich ergebend' verwendet werden:
any resulting excess profit

result Substantiv. *a result* ist ‚ein Ergebnis, Resultat' in der Folge von etwas.
The results are mathematically daunting. ... beängstigend.
The results are striking.
Similar studies have found the same results.
with striking results mit überraschenden Ergebnissen

Das Ergebnis ‚von' wird mit *of* konstruiert.
The result of this sort of competition ...

‚Das Ergebnis ist, dass ...' ist *The result is that ...;* ‚mit dem Ergebnis, dass' ist *with the result that ...* oder *as a result.*
As a result, imports are increasing ...

since. Die Konjunktion *since* bedeutet in einigen Fällen auch ‚da, weil'. Nebensätze, die mit *since* im kausalen Sinne beginnen, stehen meist vor dem Hauptsatz. Nebensatz und Hauptsatz zeigen die gleichen Verbformen *(present – present; simple past – simple past).*
Since emerging economies offer higher returns on investment than industrial economies, they are likely to enjoy a net inflow of capital ...
Die Endstellung des Nebensatzes findet sich jedoch auch:
Many people do not bother to register as unemployed, since benefits are meagre.

Wenn *since* die Bedeutung ‚seit' hat, steht im Hauptsatz meist das *present perfect,* also eine Verbform mit *have* und Partizip Perfekt. Oder der Nebensatz zeigt ein *simple past,* wie z.B. in:
Coffee prices plunged this week to their lowest level since frosts hit Brazil's coffee-growing region in late June.

so. *so* ist ‚daher, deshalb'.
Poor people cannot save much, so poor countries cannot finance the investment that is needed for them to grow.
So real exchange rates could rise with no help from capital inflows.
This would reduce the cost of labour and so encourage employers to hire extra workers.

thanks to. *thanks to* ist ein präpositionaler Ausdruck mit der Bedeutung ‚aufgrund, wegen'.
Nickel prices have doubled this year, thanks to strong demand for stainless steel.
Since 1981, America has shifted from being the world's biggest creditor to its biggest debtor, thanks to its persistent current-account deficits.

therefore Adverb. *therefore* ist ‚deshalb'. Das Adverb kann an verschiedenen Stellen im Satz stehen, jedoch nicht am Ende. Die bevorzugte Stellung ist die nach dem ersten Hilfsverb, im Falle von *have to* jedoch vor dem *have.* Weiterhin: Es steht vor einer einfachen Form von *be*. Es kann auch als Einschub zwischen Kommas gesetzt werden.

America's Federal Reserve may therefore feel obliged to lift interest rates.
Tax rates therefore have to rise at an accelerating pace.
It is therefore essential for the Clinton administration to ...
It is hard, therefore, to conclude that ...

therefore wird öfters mit einer *it is*-Einleitung verbunden.
It is therefore difficult to say ...
It is therefore essential to ...
It is therefore easier to ...
It is therefore important that ...
It is therefore likely that ...

why. *why* kann nach Wörtern wie *explain* und *reason* stehen.
This explains why the dollar has fallen by only 8% in trade-weighted terms over the past 12 months ... Das erklärt, warum ...
There are good reasons why official income indicators might underestimate the amount of money people have.

Eine Begründung kann mit *that is why* ‚aus diesem Grund, daher' eingeführt werden.
Ansonsten ist *why* das Fragewort ‚warum, weshalb'.

VALUE – WORTH

value Substantiv. Der Wert, den eine Sache hat, kann mit *value* oder *worth* bezeichnet werden. Allerdings ist *value* der ‚(finanziell ermittelbare) Wert'.
National parks and air quality are not bought or sold. It is therefore difficult to use market transactions to gauge their value. In some cases economists can decide their worth indirectly.
a decline in the value of imports
a drop in the value of the currency
Trees have a market value as timber. ... einen Marktwert als Bauholz.
How do you put a value on the environment?

value Verb. *value something* bedeutet ‚einen bestimmten finanziellen Wert beilegen', ‚einen finanziellen Wert ermitteln'.
Valuing life and safety is not as callous as it sounds. Einen finanziellen Wert für Leben und Sicherheit anzusetzen ist weniger unmenschlich ...
value something kann auch im ideellen Sinne verwendet werden.
What people value most about seeing a film ... Was die Leute am meisten schätzen, wenn sie einen Film sehen ...

worth Substantiv. Mit *net worth* bezeichnet man ‚Reinvermögen/Eigenkapital' (also *assets minus liabilities*).
Many patents never reach the market, making it hard to assess their worth.
‚Im Wert von' kann mit *-worth* konstruiert werden.
buying $235 billion-worth of goods

Mit *worth* wird auch ein Wert bezeichnet, der nicht oder nicht nur finanziell zu sehen ist: *a forest's worth* (der Wert eines Waldes) liegt auch in der Funktion der Naherholung oder in der Wirkung auf das lokale Klima.

worth Adjektiv. *worth* wird mit Ergänzungen verwendet.
bonds worth DM 1 billion
A dollar invested at 10% will be worth six times as much a century from now as a dollar invested at 8%.
40 cents in 1800 is worth more than $4 in today's money.

Wenn etwas einen bestimmten Aufwand lohnt, dann ist es *worth something*. Die Ergänzung kann auch in der *ing*-Form eines Verbs bestehen.
It may be worth the cost.
It could still be worth doing.
This discussion is worth revisiting. Es wird sich lohnen, auf diese Diskussion zurückzukommen.

VERGLEICH, ÄHNLICHKEIT, UNTERSCHIED

Siehe hierzu auch den Abschnitt STEIGEN, MEHR WERDEN ..., dort besonders die Teilabschnitte „4. Schneller" und „5. Langsamer", ferner den Abschnitt GEGENSATZ, EINRÄUMUNG.

Adjektive, Adverbien. Siehe auch *than* und *as ... as* in diesem Abschnitt. Die häufigsten Adjektive/Adverbien, die in der Konstruktion mit *than* verwendet werden, sind *better, faster, more favourable, greater, higher, keener, larger, less, longer, lower, more moderate, more rapidly, smaller, slower, more slowly, more steeply, stronger, tighter, weaker, worse.*

***as**. as* ‚wie' leitet Nebensätze ein, die davon handeln, dass jemand etwas gesagt, gezeigt hat, oft im Rahmen einer Argumentation.
As a recent analysis by another British securities firm, SG Warburg, points out ...
... as Mr Kay admits.
as David Currie argues ...

as it stands ist ‚wie die Dinge liegen'. Der Einschub *as it were* ist ‚sozusagen'.

Als Präposition wird *as* gebraucht, um zu sagen, dass etwas ‚als' oder ‚wie' etwas gesehen oder beschrieben wird, oder verwendet wird. Also vor allem nach Verben wie *be seen, be used, be treated, be regarded* usw.
Britain's shift from income tax to VAT has been perceived as a move to lower taxes.
The model should be seen as a gross underestimate of the fruits of liberalisation.

as vor einer Berufsbezeichnung ist ‚(in der Eigenschaft) als'.
as a politician ... als Politiker

Weitere Kombinationen sind:
just as genau so wie
as ever wie sonst
as usual wie üblich

as ... as. Mit *as ... as* wird der Vergleich ‚so ... wie' formuliert. Zwischen den beiden *as* steht ein Adjektiv oder ein Adverb (in der Grundform).
as fast as possible
This recession was not as deep as those in the mid -1970s.
In particular, why is Western Europe's unemployment rate, at almost 12%, twice as high as America's?
... three times as many as in France ...
Japan and Germany are both international creditors, but neither has an economy as large as America's ...

Bei der Verneinung wird *not* davor gesetzt.
In other words, Japan's fiscal policy is not as loose as it seems.
This belief is not as silly as it seems.

Adjektive oder Adverbien nach dem ersten *as* können weiter ergänzt werden.
Product-market barriers may be as much to blame as labour-market rigidities for Western Europe's high rate of unemployment.
... sind vielleicht im selben Maße verantwortlich ...

as if, as though. *as if* oder *as though* leitet einen als-ob-Vergleich ein. Die entsprechenden Sätze zeigen meist *were* statt *was*.
Such statistical oddities encourage policy-makers to behave as though natural wealth were limitless. ... als ob die natürlichen Ressourcen unbegrenzt seien.
Their strongest argument is that the owners behaved as if there were no tomorrow.
... dass sich die Eigentümer so verhielten, als gäbe es kein Morgen.

comparable. Das Adjektiv *comparable* ['kɒmprəbl] ist ‚vergleichbar'.
No comparable study has been done in America.

Der Gegenstand des Vergleiches wird mit *to* angeschlossen.
... growth in the 1980s was at least comparable to growth in the first 80 years of this century.

comparative. Das Adjektiv *comparative* ist ‚vergleichend'. Unter *comparative advertising* versteht man die ‚vergleichende Werbung'.

Das Adverb hierzu ist *comparatively* ‚vergleichsweise'.
a comparatively young technology

compare Verb. Mit *compare* wird das Vergleichen bezeichnet.

Die Konstruktion *compare with* (ohne Objekt) entspricht ‚x lässt sich vergleichen mit, ist vergleichbar mit'
These compare with a 32% plunge over the past three months.

compare wird auch konstruiert als *compare + something (+ with something/+ to something)*
A popular way to compare different shares is to look at their price/earnings ratios.

A price/earnings (p/e) ratio is a useful guide to investors' attitudes. It compares a firm's share price with its earnings per share.

Am häufigsten findet sich diese Konstruktion in der Form eines Nebensatzes, und bedeutet dann soviel wie ‚verglichen mit ... / ... verglichen mit'.

... their average forecast for January 1994 is DM 1.73, compared with the current DM 1.61.

But only 3,000 wildcat miners are digging at the mine, compared with 20,000 a year ago.

Compared with other emerging equity markets the sub-Saharan region is tiny.

Im Sinne von ‚Man vergleiche ..., Vergleiche ...' wird der Imperativ verwendet.

Compare the German experience with that of Poland.

Der Anschluss mit *to* statt *with* ist selten.

Optimists now outnumber pessimists there by 82%, compared to only 17% in the first quarter of this year.

comparison Substantiv. *a comparison* ist ein Vergleich (verschiedener Phänomene).

Such comparisons are meaningless.

Das ‚mit' wird durch *with* ausgedrückt.

Many people make comparisons with Argentina, which has had remarkable success against inflation ...

Das ‚von' wird durch *of* ausgedrückt.

on the basis of a detailed comparison of prices in each country auf der Grundlage eines detaillierten Preisvergleichs ...

Eine Darstellung ‚zum Vergleich' ist *for comparison*. (Die Darstellung selbst ist ein *ranking*).

The chart ranks ERM members (along with Britain and Italy for comparison) ...

Die Art des Vergleiches kann vor dem *comparison* stehen.

Germany, by contrast, continues to lag behind even on an industry-by-industry comparison.

Die Fügung *by comparison* ist ‚im Vergleich (hierzu)'.

By comparison, America's budget deficit of 'only' 4.3% of GDP looks relatively modest.

difference. *difference* ist ‚Unterschied, Verschiedenheit', es kann im Singular und Plural verwendet werden. ‚Unterschied(e) zwischen' wird mit *between* formuliert.
the difference between America and Europe
the differences between companies

Wenn von einem Bereich die Rede ist, der in sich Verschiedenheiten aufweist, spricht man von *differences in something*.
international differences in prices
the differences in productivity levels
differences in the types of capital

it makes no/little difference (to somebody) es macht keinen/wenig Unterschied (für jemanden)
the difference is that ... Der Unterschied liegt darin, dass

different. *different* ist ‚verschiedenartig, verschieden, unterschiedlich'.
different types of schools
a different view
different parts of society
Japan is different.

‚verschieden von' ist *different from*.
Many reckon that this is little different from floating.
Import penetration today is not very different from what it was in the 1960s. Die Importquote ...

even. Vor einem Komparativ kann *even* in der Bedeutung ‚(sogar) noch' stehen.
In real terms, of course, the fall is even sharper.
Product-market barriers may be even more important than labour-market rigidities.

example. ‚Beispiel' kann mit *example* ausgedrückt werden. Geeignete Beispiele sind *classic, famous, handy, prime examples*, ‚weitere Beispiele' *further examples*.
Forests are a good example.
The example of the European Union ... suggests that ...
There are examples of specific projects that have done a lot of good.
Mr Scherer gives several examples of how this happens.

‚zum Beispiel' ist *for instance* oder *for example*.
For example, the Economic Outlook shows that the average inflation rate in the OECD fell from 7.8% in 1987 to 4.2% in 1994.
... in most countries, for example, utilities are still state monopolies. ... liegt die Versorgung (mit Wasser, Gas usw.) in den Händen von Staatsmonopolen.

further. *further* vor Substantiven bedeutet ‚weiter-, zusätzlich'. Das Adverb *further* bedeutet ‚weiterhin', oft ‚weiter in der angegebenen Richtung, Tendenz'.
... assuming a further increase, to 6.7%.
two further articles by economists
further examples of dramatic expansion of farm exports.
Only Warsaw, which leapt by 11.2%, rose further.
Optimists go further still. Optimisten gehen noch weiter.

Komparativ. Der Komparativ ist die Form des Adjektivs oder Adverbs, wie sie vor *than* steht, z.B. *smaller than ..., less expensive than ..., more rigidly than ...* Adjektive im Komparativ können (auch ohne Vergleichskonstruktion) vor Substantiven stehen - wie im Deutschen:
bigger losses größere Verluste
smaller firms kleinere Firmen

less. Die Komparativkonstruktion mit *less* und *than* ist ‚weniger als'.
Long-term youth unemployment is less than 10% in America, Canada, Japan and Sweden, but more than 40% in Italy, Ireland, Spain and Belgium.
Copper stocks are down to less than six weeks' consumption.

less vor Adjektiven und Adverbien ist ‚weniger'.
Unfortunately, as a result, some of the aggregate figures have become less useful.

less of ist ‚weniger an, von'
If foreigners held less of their wealth in dollars ...

more or less ist ‚mehr oder weniger'.
... its share of developing countries' reserves has stayed more or less flat since 1980.
But its farmers have grown less sugar ... weniger Zucker angebaut.

Siehe auch den Abschnitt *LITTLE - SMALL*.

like. Wenn gesagt wird, *A is like B,* dann sind *A* und *B* einander ähnlich, vergleichbar. Bevorzugte Verben sind *be, look, sound.*
These examples are, in a way, just like games.
That looks like a bonanza. Das sieht nach einer Goldgrube aus.

like bedeutet auch, dass etwas ‚wie etwas gemacht, gehandhabt' werden soll.
Infrastructure should be run like a business.

like mit Substantiv (nach einem Substantiv) ist ‚wie (auch)'.
Members of the Currency School, like later monetarists, emphasised the monetary causes of inflation. ... wie auch spätere Monetaristen ...
non-monetary assets like bonds ... wie z.B. Schuldverschreibungen
The Fund, like most forecasters, has recently had a poor track record.
Governments, like voters, are naturally more interested in short-term than long-term growth.
in an economy like Japan's ... wie der in Japan

and the like ist ‚und ähnliche(s)'.
credit guarantees and the like

many – much. Hierzu siehe den Abschnitt *MANY – MUCH.*

more. Mit *more* wird der Komparativ von (fast allen) Adverbien gebildet.
All of these markets could emerge even more dramatically.
America's yield curve is sloping upwards much more steeply than a year ago.
Die wichtigste Ausnahme ist *faster* ‚schneller'.
... the output of Japan's industry has grown faster than that of any other of the seven largest OECD members.

more wird auch zur Bildung des Komparativs von Adjektiven verwendet. Dieses *more* haben alle drei- und mehrsilbigen Adjektive und fast alle zweisilbigen Adjektive (sofern sie nicht auf *-y* enden, wie z.B. *silly, dirty, happy, easy).*
Forecasters are becoming more nervous about Australia's rapid growth.
more generous welfare payments
Its curve is more inverted.

more ist der Komparativ zum Adverb *much.*
But that does not mean that everything costs more.
That average conceals more than it reveals.
But Hong Kong, Sao Paulo and Moscow all gained more than 3% in the week.

The price of water in most countries has more to do with politics than with the economic cost of providing it. ... hat mehr mit Politik zu tun als ...

‚viel mehr' als adverbiale Bestimmung ist *much more*.
Japanese companies, however, have focused much more on Asia. ... haben sich viel stärker auf Asien konzentriert.

Vor Substantiven ist *more* ‚mehr'.
America invested even more money abroad than Japan.

‚mehr an, mehr von' vor Substantiven ist *more of*.
... as more of the current crop will be available for export.

or more ist ‚oder mehr', *more or less* ist ‚mehr oder weniger'.
Santiago, Singapore and Istanbul also managed increases of 3% or more.
Its share of developing countries' reserves has stayed more or less flat since 1980.

same. *same* tritt zusammen mit dem bestimmten Artikel *the* auf und wird im Sinne von ‚der-/die-/dasselbe, der, die, das gleiche' verwendet.
Will the dollar suffer the same fate?
the same amount of money
the same inflationary impact
at the same time zur gleichen Zeit
in the same way auf die gleiche Weise

Ähnlich wie im Deutschen kann *the same* auch ohne folgendes Substantiv verwendet werden (also als Pronomen).
Other studies have found the same. ... haben das Gleiche ermittelt.
The same goes for X Das Gleiche trifft auf X zu.
The same is true in Japan.

The same kann nach dem Verb *cost,* nach *be* und nach anderen Verben stehen, die einen Zustand oder ein Werden beschreiben.
Both cost the same.
10 years ago they were roughly the same.

Das *the same* kann mit vorgestelltem *exactly* betont werden, mit *roughly* abgeschwächt werden.
the two groups, roughly the same in population ... ... von ungefähr der gleichen Bevölkerungszahl ...

seem. Mit *seem* wird ausgedrückt, dass etwas irgendwie zu sein scheint.
Nach *seem to be* steht eine Konstruktion mit einem Substantiv, einem Adjektiv (oder einer adverbialen Bestimmung wie in *This seems to be in order*).
There did indeed seem to be a link between gold prices and inflation.
This seems to be the case regardless of the political system.
Capital-market barriers seem to be unimportant, even for small firms.

Das *to be* kann ausgelassen werden.
To many Britons this may seem perverse.
Sometimes, surveys record preferences that seem inconsistent with reasonable behaviour. ... die mit vernünftigem Verhalten nicht im Einklang zu stehen scheinen.
asking what may seem a dull question

seem to + Verb. *Seem* kann mit einem Infinitiv mit *to* weitergeführt werden.
Aid flows seem to have no impact on infant mortality rates.
Worries about American inflation caused European markets to slip, but seemed not to trouble Wall Street. ... schienen aber Wall Street nicht zu beunruhigen

it seems that. *It seems ... that* ist ‚Es scheint ..., dass'.
It may seem intuitively appealing that rich countries should give money to poorer ones to help them grow faster and live better.
It seems unlikely that ...
It seems that people in most African and Latin American countries are living for longer and in better conditions.

‚wie es scheint' ist *as it seems*.
Japan's fiscal policy is not as loose as it seems.

it seems kann, zwischen Kommas, an verschiedenen Stellen des Satzes als ‚wie es scheint' gesetzt werden.

similar. Das Adjektiv *similar* bezeichnet Ähnlichkeit.
similar arguments
The story in Africa is similar.
Several similar studies have found the same results.

Wenn eine Sache/Person einer anderen ähnlich ist, verwendet man *similar to*.
a payments union, similar to the one in Western Europe eine Zahlungsunion, ähnlich der im westlichen Europa
The extent of such barriers in Japan is similar to that in America.

similarly. Das Adverb *similarly* entspricht dem Adverb ‚ähnlich'.
a similarly strong role
Meistens jedoch steht es am Satzanfang, durch Komma vom Rest getrennt, und bedeutet dann ‚in ähnlicher Weise'.
Similarly, much of East Asia's recent economic success has been based on investment in human capital.

similarity. *similarity* ist ‚Ähnlichkeit'. Es kann im Plural gebraucht werden. Dem ‚zwischen' entspricht *between*.
But here the similarities end.
It is not the similarities between firms that matter, but the differences – specifically those that explain why some firms succeed and others fail.

so. *so* vor Adjektiven oder Adverbien ist ‚derart'.
The real puzzle is why the dollar's international role is so big.
Zu *even so* siehe *even* in GEGENSATZ, EINRÄUMUNG.

still. Vor Komparativen bedeutet *still* ‚noch (mehr)'.
And the higher interest rate might then attract still more foreign capital, making matters worse. ... könnte dann noch mehr ausländisches Kapital anziehen und so die Lage verschlimmern.
Aber auch die Bedeutung ‚immer noch' ist anzutreffen.
But so far as inflation-fighting is concerned, it is still better to be roughly right than precisely wrong.
Siehe auch ZEIT, dort „2.4 Gleichzeitigkeit".

Am Satzanfang kommen *worse still* und *better still* vor, ‚schlimmer noch', ‚besser noch'.
Worse still, much of the spending has gone to waste.

such. *such* ist ‚solch-‘ und greift vorher Erwähntes wieder auf. Mit unbestimmtem Artikel ist es *such a.* Bei Betonung des unbestimmten Artikels (‚EIN solcher‘) heißt es *one such.* Der bestimmte Artikel wird nicht verwendet. Bei Substantiven, die im grammatischen Sinne nicht zählbar sind, steht *such* alleine.
Such differences are largely explained by funds' investment patterns.
Such big differences between trade statistics produced by different sources ...
Such a code need not, at least at first, be very detailed.
One such study took two groups of deer-hunters.
Such instability would harm the whole world economy.

such as führt ein oder mehrere Beispiele ein.
In countries with apprenticeship systems, such as Austria, Germany and Switzerland. In Ländern mit einem Lehrlingsausbildungssystem, wie Österreich ...

Superlativ. Superlative sind Formen des Adjektivs wie *biggest* (zu *big*) oder *most generous* (zu *generous*). Oder Formen des Adverbs wie *most dramatically, most steeply.*
America was the world's biggest creditor until the early 1980s. ... der größte Gläubiger ...
Argentina is the largest of them.
These are biggest in countries whose unemployment benefits are high ... ... am größten ...

than. *than* ist Teil der Komparativkonstruktion, wie etwa in *more than 3%,* ‚mehr als 3%‘. Vor dem *than* muss stets ein Komparativ stehen, wie *more, higher* oder *more highly.* Dieser Komparativ muss aber nicht unmittelbar vorangehen. *than* braucht anschließend stets eine Ergänzung. Siehe auch ‚Adjektive, Adverbien‘ in diesem Abschnitt.
Bombay lost more than 5%.
The Soviet Union may have more than 200,000 tonnes of uranium in stock.
2.5% higher than a year ago
They have been keener than Americans and Japanese to invest.
down by more than half from 7.8%
more than in 1997
a quarter more than in the West

Folgt nach dem *than* noch ein Satz, können Teile dieses Satzes ausgelassen werden.
Americans eat far more fast food than people in other developed countries [ausgelassen: *eat* bzw. *do*]

even than verwendet man, wenn man ‚sogar noch' ausdrücken will.
a rate higher even than Italy's

other than ist ‚andere als' oder ‚Nicht-':
in currencies other than sterling

rather than ist ‚statt, anstatt, bevor':
The money might be better spent supporting new democratic governments rather than trying to give to the poor over a long period. ... anstatt zu versuchen, ...

too. Vor Adjektiven und Adverbien drückt *too* ein Übermaß aus, ‚zu'.
Generous minimum wages and jobless benefits keep wages too high at the lower end of the pay spectrum.
Such a conclusion is too hasty.

Wenn das Adjektiv vor einem folgenden Substantiv steht, wird der unbestimmte Artikel umgestellt.
But most such schemes have collapsed, mainly because they attempted to support prices at too high a level ... ... auf einem zu hohen Niveau ...

Die entsprechende Konstruktion mit dem bestimmten Artikel *the* gibt es nicht.

too kann auch im Sinne von ‚ebenfalls' verwendet werden.
They too have thrown in the towel and embraced the policy.
Producers gained too (which is surprising), to the tune of $3 billion a year.
But she is unrealistic about governments; they fail too ...
This too is possible.

way. *way* kann im Sinne von Möglichkeit oder im Sinne von ‚Art und Weise (wie)' verwendet werden. Es ist meist Bestandteil von Konstruktionen aus mehreren Wörtern.
a/the (...) way to...
A popular way to compare different shares is to look at their price/earnings ratios. Eine übliche Methode ...
‚Aid fatigue' is a fashionable way to describe the increasing reluctance of rich countries to give foreign aid to poor ones. ... ist derzeit eine gängige Art ...
Greater private involvement is a better way to sharpen efficiency.
the best way to judge people's tastes

Konstruiert wird folgendermaßen: *a/the* + Adjektiv + *way* + *to* mit Infinitiv oder *a/the* + Adjektiv + *way* + *of* + verb-*ing*. Und auch *a/the* + Adjektiv + *way* + *for someone* + *to* mit Infinitiv.
The best way for a firm to do that is to promote its own standard.

Weitere Wendungen:
in the same way auf dieselbe Weise
in some ways in gewisser Weise, in mancher Hinsicht
in this way auf diese Weise
in much the same way auf sehr ähnliche Weise
either way ob man es nun auf diese Weise oder auf die andere Weise sieht
in a way in gewisser Weise
in a way that auf eine Art und Weise, die ...
in just the same way auf ebensolche Weise
seen this way so gesehen
in such a way as to ... dergestalt, dass
[They] altered the structure of the financial system in such a way as to make the rules fail.

WERTPAPIERE

In diesem Abschnitt werden behandelt: *assets – asset, securities – security, equities – equity, stocks – stock, shares – share, bonds – bond, funds – fund.*

assets/asset. Mit *assets* bezeichnet man das Vermögen/das Eigentum eines Unternehmens, einer Person oder eines Landes. Mit wenigen Ausnahmen ordnen sich alle anderen oben genannten Termini (*equities* usw.) unter *assets* ein.
assets kommt u.a. in den folgenden Ausdrücken und Kontexten vor:
assets and liabilities Aktiva und Passiva
fixed assets Anlagevermögen
net foreign assets Nettoauslandsforderungen
household/personal assets Privatvermögen
(the) age, sex, background and assets of the self-employed Vermögen
environmental assets, such as forests and mineral deposits (hier etwa im Sinne von) Naturschätze

assets können näher bestimmt werden durch Modifikation wie etwa *higher-yielding, interest-bearing, profitable, risky/riskier, safe.*
shifting bank deposits into higher-yielding assets such as mutual funds ... Anlagen mit höheren Renditen ...

assets erscheint oft mit den folgenden Verben oder deren -*ing* Form als Substantiv:
to buy, to hold, to invest in, to sell, to trade, to value.
the kinds of assets that banks could hold
to stop investing in fixed assets, such as property
... if a firm were shut down and its assets sold ...
valuing the government's assets was no easy task.

In wirtschaftlichen Texten kommt der Singular *asset* seltener vor als der Plural; er erscheint oft in Komposita.
... by buying an asset whose value rises.
gold or some other liquid asset flüssige Mittel
the slump (Rückgang) *in asset prices*
capital-asset pricing model (CAPM) Kapitalanlagepreis-Modell

Die allgemeinsprachliche Bedeutung von *asset* im Sinne von Vorteil kommt weniger häufig vor.
Personen, die als *assets to the firm* bezeichnet werden, sind gute Mitarbeiter.

securities – security. *securities* ist der Sammelbegriff für Wertpapiere. Hauptsächlich werden damit Aktien *(shares)* und Anleihen *(bonds)* bezeichnet.
The prices of such securities will be volatile. ... sind Veränderungen unterworfen.
higher yields on securities höhere Wertpapierrenditen
a London securities firm Börsenmaklerfirma
Government securities Staatspapiere
the Securities and Exchange Commission (SEC) die Börsenaufsichtsbehörde (der USA)

securities werden oft beschrieben als:
fixed-interest securities festverzinsliche Wertpapiere
gilt-edged securities Staatspapiere (UK)
listed securities börsennotierte Wertpapiere

In diesem Sinne wird auch der Singular manchmal verwendet:
the interest rate on a 'risk-free' security

Jedoch bedeutet der Singular *security* meistens ‚Sicherheit', wie in den folgenden Beispielen:

the link between job security and training der Zusammenhang zwischen Sicherheit des Arbeitsplatzes und Ausbildung
the national security of the United States

In Kombination mit *social* bezieht sich *security* auf das Sozialversicherungswesen:
social security contributions Beiträge zur Sozialversicherung
social security benefits Sozialleistungen

equities/equity. *equities/equity* bedeuten je nach Kontext, entweder ‚Aktien' oder ‚Eigenkapital' im Gegensatz zu ‚Fremdkapital' (d.h. *debt or outside capital*).
Measures of the cost of equity are more controversial. ... Eigenkapitalkosten ...
Japanese firms enjoy vastly cheaper equity finance. ... Finanzierung über Aktien
according to the debt-equity ratio ... Verschuldungsgrad
America's bond and equity markets ... Wertpapierbörsen
.. raise more finance by issuing debt and equity ... durch Emission von Schuldverschreibungen und Aktien
After the 1987 crash, when equities lost a fifth of their value ...

equity bildet Komposita mit *stake(s)* und *holding(s)* im Sinne von Kapitalbeteiligung(en).
.. with managers owning a large equity stake
94% of their equity holdings in domestic securities Inlandswerte

stocks/stock. *stocks/stock,* können, je nach Kontext, verschiedenes bedeuten; die meisten dieser Bedeutungen ordnen sich dem Oberbegriff *assets* unter.

Die Komposita mit *exchange* oder *market* sind allgemein geläufig.
the New York Stock Exchange (NYSE) New Yorker Börse
Stock markets rallied on Friday. Die Börsen erholten sich ...

Im engeren Sinne bedeutet *stock(s)* ‚Aktien' im Gegensatz zu *bonds* ‚Anleihen'.
Toronto stocks weakened on Friday.
pharmaceutical and oil stocks Pharma- und Erdölwerte
an underlying asset such as a stock or bond
They over-invest in ‚hot' stocks. ... in Spekulationswerten

stock kommt auch manchmal als Sammelbegriff vor.
[They] acquired CWT Inc. for about $1.5 billion in stock.
.. by selling stock to many dispersed investors.

stock wird nicht mit dem unbestimmten Artikel oder im Plural verwendet, wie es bei *share(s)* der Fall ist, um eine oder mehrere Aktien eines bestimmten Unternehmens zu bezeichnen. *They bought 1000 shares of Daimler Benz.* Aber: *They own some BMW stock.*

stocks/stock kann auch Vorräte/Lagerbestände/Menge bedeuten:
Companies today keep much leaner stocks than in the past.
by maintaining a buffer stock ... Pufferbestand
the total monetary stock in Russia ... Geldmenge ...

stock + *of* + Substantiv kommt auch im allgemeinsprachlichen Sinne von ‚Menge' vor.
to accumulate a stock of wealth for their old age. ein gewisses Vermögen

stock als Verb:
Retailers stock a manufacturer's whole range. ... führen ...

shares/share. *shares/share* haben, ähnlich wie *stocks-stock,* verschiedene Bedeutungen. Am häufigsten wird *share(s)* im Sinne von ‚Aktien' benutzt, ob alleinstehend oder in Komposita.
EGT Inc. shares jumped 15 percent on Monday.
More people now own homes and shares.
... when a share of IBM sold for around $110.
employee share ownership schemes/plans ... Belegschaftsaktien-Programme
falling/rising share prices ... Aktienkurse

In Kombination mit *market* erscheint *share(s)* als ‚Marktanteil(e)'.
... losing market share to newcomers. ... und verlor Marktanteile an neue Konkurrenten.
Its world market shares have improved in most areas of its business.

Im Sinne von ‚Anteil' kommt *share* sehr oft mit *of* + Substantiv vor.
the budget deficit as a share of GDP
The share of manufacturing has fallen ...
Columbia's share of world coffee production.

Das Verb *to share* bedeutet ‚teilen' oder ‚sich beteiligen':
... to share their know-how.
... to share some of the costs.

bonds/bond. *bonds/bond* sind langfristige, festverzinsliche Schuldverschreibungen.
Bonds can be issued by governments and firms. von der öffentlichen Hand und von Unternehmen ausgegeben
bond yields Anleiherenditen
long-term bond langfristige Anleihe
government bonds Staatsschuldverschreibungen
30-year U.S. treasury bonds dreißigjährige Staatsanleihe
mortgage bonds Pfandbriefe
junk bonds minderwertige Anleihen
the bond market Rentenmarkt

funds/fund. *funds/fund* gleichen häufig den deutschen ‚Fonds':
the International Monetary Fund (IMF) Internationaler Währungs-Fonds (IWF)
... invested by banks and pension funds ... Pensionsfonds
a money-market mutual fund Geldmarkt-Investmentfonds

Manchmal bezeichnet *funds,* nur im Plural, finanzielle Mittel, Gelder oder Kapital.
public funds öffentliche Mittel
the international competition for funds ... Kapital
the federal funds/fedfunds rate (Federal Reserve, USA) Tagesgeldsatz

WILL – WOULD

Aussagen in Bezug auf die Zukunft werden im Englischen in der Regel mit Modalverben formuliert (z.B. mit *will, can, could, may, might, must*) oder mit Umschreibung wie *be going to, be bound to, be about to*). Das Präsens dient nur in wenigen Fällen zur Bezeichnung für die Zukunft: Man verwendet es, wenn man über Ereignisse spricht, die als unabänderlich angesehen werden, wie z.B. *Tomorrow the sun sets at 7.32 pm* oder *The boat leaves at 3.40 am.* (Diese Art der „Zukunfts-Gewissheit" ist aber in wirtschaftlichen Texten nicht gegeben.)

will. Mit *will* drückt man aus, dass etwas so sein wird, normale Umstände sowie die Fähigkeit zur Einschätzung vorausgesetzt. Man ist also relativ zuversichtlich und operiert nicht mit ‚kann, könnte, müsste, sollte' usw. *will* wird in *that*-Sätzen ver-

wendet, die sich auf Einschätzungen (Hoffnungen, Befürchtungen, Schlüsse) beziehen. Im Deutschen steht das Präsens oder die Umschreibung mit ‚werden'.
Next spring America will enter its fifth year of recovery.
Growth will be more evenly spread.
How quickly will higher interest rates dampen demand?
The OECD believes that this slowdown will be enough to prevent a sharp pick-up in inflation.
They fear that higher rates will strangle investment in the developed world.
Its analysis concludes that there will be a significant increase in household savings.
Michael Howell, research director at Baring Securities, predicts that by 2010 emerging markets will account for 40-45% of global stockmarket capitalisation, up from 15% today.

Bei *if*-Sätzen mit dem Präsens steht im Hauptsatz *will*. Ebenso bei Sätzen mit *unless* oder *when*.
This means that in the early stages of recovery inflation will continue to slow, even if output is growing above the trend.
If the jobless rate is higher than this, inflation will slow; if lower, it will accelerate.
When output is below its potential, inflation will slow or stay muted.

In Nebensätzen, die mit einer „zeitlichen" Konjunktion beginnen, steht kein *will*.
Bidders start with a low initial bid and then raise their bids until a winner emerges.
... und erhöhen dann den Preis, bis sich ein Gewinner herausstellt.
Until inflation gets well above 5%, this cost is not huge.

In einigen Zusammenhängen kann *will* auch ‚Absicht' bedeuten oder es kann eine Art Absichtskomponente enthalten sein.
It is still not known when, or if, China will join.
Britain will now offer firms subsidies when they hire someone who has been out of work for over two years. ... Subventionen

will always bedeutet ‚ist/sind immer (weil es eben so ist)'.
Italian politicians will always be reluctant to take unpopular measures.

Die Umschreibung mit *going to* ist in formellen Texten sehr selten.
Unfortunately that is not going to happen any time soon.

Zu *be about to* siehe den Abschnitt *ABOUT*.

Mit *will have* und dem Partizip Perfekt wird eine relativ starke Gewissheit ausgedrückt, dass etwas, zu einem Zeitpunkt in der Zukunft, eingetreten sein wird. Diese Konstruktion findet sich in Wirtschaftstexten nur selten.

would. Mit *would* wird ausgedrückt, dass etwas (unter bestimmten Umständen) so wäre, dass jemand etwas tun würde – also Mutmaßungen, Hoffnungen, Erwartungen, Befürchtungen.
That would be a good start. Das wäre ein guter Anfang.
How much would you be willing to pay? Wieviel wären Sie bereit zu zahlen?
Such instability would harm the whole world economy – not just America. ... würde der gesamten Weltwirtschaft schaden ...
Few believed that they would be exposed to competition.
Dementsprechend steht *would* in *that*-Sätzen, die sich auf Behauptungen, Hoffnungen, Befürchtungen beziehen.
Stockmarkets stumbled this week because of fears that strong economic growth would prompt central banks in America and Britain to raise interest rates again.
... dass ein starkes Wirtschaftswachstum die Zentralbanken in Amerika und Großbritannien dazu veranlassen würde, ...

Bei *if*-Sätzen, die im *past tense* stehen, steht *would* im Hauptsatz.
Would you want a particular programme to be enacted if you had to pay dollars X for it? Würden Sie ein bestimmtes Programm realisiert sehen wollen, wenn Sie dafür x Dollar zahlen müssten?
Even if they promised to do so, there would be no way of holding them to their word. Auch wenn sie es versprächen – es gäbe keine Möglichkeit, dieses Versprechen einzufordern.

Mit Verben des Sagens im *past tense* (die die indirekte Rede einleiten) steht *would*, wenn in der direkten Rede *will* steht.
VW announced that it would make no further comments on the dispute.
Hier hat VW verlautbart: *"We will make no further comments ..."* Wegen des *announced* muss aber dann in der indirekten Rede *would* stehen, also „VW sagte, dass man keine weiteren Kommentare zu dieser Auseinandersetzung abgeben werde."

Karl Marx hoped that communism would mean the end of money. ... dass der Kommunismus das Ende der Geldwirtschaft sein werde.
a voucher promising that the state would pay part of their wage if they found a job ein(e Art) Gutschein, mit der Garantie, dass der Staat einen Teil des Lohnes zahlen werde, wenn sie einen Arbeitsplatz finden.

would rather und *would sooner* bedeuten, dass es jemandem lieber wäre, wenn ..., dass jemand vorzieht, etwas zu tun.

VW has, perfectly legally, acquired lots of information about its rival that GM would rather it did not have. ... eine Menge von Information über seinen Konkurrenten, die General Motors lieber nicht in Händen von VW sähe.
Most Americans remain baffled that Europeans would rather have their exchange rates managed by bureaucrats than by the market. ... dass Europäer es vorziehen, die Wechselkurse ...
Big firms ask economists to predict the ups and downs of national economies, but when it comes to finding ways to run their own company better, many managers would sooner consult an astrologer. ... dann wenden sich viele Manager eher an einen Astrologen.

Jemand, der ein *would-be X* ist, ist ein potentieller X: *a would-be rival, a would-be competitor.*

would have. would have mit Partizip Perfekt bedeutet, dass etwas in der Vergangenheit der Fall gewesen wäre, geschehen wäre.
A couple of years ago this would have sounded like fiction. Vor zwei Jahren hätte man das noch als unrealistisch empfunden.
Some workers would have found jobs even without a subsidy. ... hätten auch ohne Unterstützung Arbeit gefunden.
Governments that receive aid in one area can use elsewhere the money they would have otherwise spent themselves ... das sie sonst anderweitig auch ausgegeben hätten.
It is difficult to know how differently they would have fared without it. ... wie es ihnen ohne das ergangen wäre.

Steht im *if-Satz* das *past perfect* (im Beispiel: *had been applied*), hat der Hauptsatz *would have* mit Partizip Perfekt.
The study compared what each creditor would have expected to get if strict legal priority had been applied with what they actually got. ... was jeder Gläubiger zu erwarten gehabt hätte, wenn eine strikte gesetzliche Priorität angewendet worden wäre.

WISSENSCHAFT UND FORSCHUNG

In diesem Abschnitt werden Wörter und Ausdrücke behandelt, die zum Bereich „Wirtschaft als Gegenstand von Forschung/Wissenschaft" gehören. Siehe hierzu auch die Abschnitte URSACHEN, FOLGEN, BEGRÜNDUNGEN und VERGLEICH, ÄHNLICHKEIT, UNTERSCHIED sowie ERWARTEN, SCHÄTZEN, VORAUSSAGEN.

academic. Das Adjektiv *academic* bezieht sich auf eher theoretische Forschungen durch Universitäten, Institute (im Unterschied zu dem, was „Praktiker" ermitteln). Dort arbeitende Forscher/Forscherinnen sind *academics*.
academics rather than practitioners
a new study by academics at the London Business School
a group of academic and business economists

academic kann auch im Sinne von ‚(etwas zu) theoretisch, akademisch' verwendet werden.
somewhat academic

article (book, paper). Wissenschaftliche Ergebnisse werden als *articles* in Zeitschriften oder Büchern veröffentlicht. *papers* sind meist kürzere Beiträge, vor allem ursprüngliche Konferenzbeiträge.
Die Verfasser werden mit *by* eingeführt.
a paper by Jagdish Bhagwati
a new book by Nicholas Lardy

Der Gegenstand der Veröffentlichung wird mit *on* eingeführt.
a flood of books on management
a forthcoming book on the FCC bidding scheme
the article on Keynes

ask. Das Verb *ask* bedeutet, in der Konstruktion *ask someone something,* ‚fragen'. Mit entsprechendem Objekt kann es ‚untersuchen' bedeuten. Die Konstruktion ist dann *ask* mit *wh*-Satz.
The study then asks how much the region can expect to receive.
The IIE study is the most thorough. It first asks how much foreign capital would be needed to raise the amount of productive capital per worker in Eastern Europe.

Hinweis. Die häufige Konstruktion *ask someone to do something* bedeutet ‚etwas von jemandem verlangen'.
Big firms ask economists to predict the ups and downs ... ... verlangen von den Wirtschaftswissenschaftlern, dass sie ...

claim Verb. *claim,* meist mit einem nachfolgenden *that-*Satz, ist ‚behaupten'. Ebenfalls möglich ist nachfolgendes *to* plus *have* plus Partizip Perfekt.
But Peter Garber, an economist at Brown University in Rhode Island, claims in a new study that ...
The IMF claims that the world economy is poised to recover. ... dass eine Erholung der Weltwirtschaft bevorstehe
McKinsey claims to have found evidence that ...

claim wird wie ein Verb des Sagens verwendet, also z.B. *it is claimed that ...,* oder *..., he claims, ...* ‚wie er behauptet' oder mit Umstellung.
Competition, or the lack of it, is one reason, claims the study.

claim Substantiv. *claim* ‚Behauptung' kann mit einem *that-*Satz ergänzt werden.
The claim that a lowish minimum wage may raise employment is not nonsense.
the claim that foreign competition is to blame for falling real wages

develop. *develop* (mit den Formen *developing* und *developed*) wird am häufigsten verwendet um zu sagen, dass sich etwas entwickelt, zu etwas wird.
developed and developing countries

Mit *develop* und *development* kann aber auch der wissenschaftlich-technologische Prozess der Herstellung bezeichnet werden.
the development of cheap vaccines die Entwicklung billiger Impfstoffe
a company which has developed a particular technology
research and development (R&D) Forschung und Entwicklung

define. *define* ‚definieren' wird als *define something (as something)* konstruiert.
This is another rationale for defining price stability as an annual inflation rate of 1-2%.
In the private sector the value of an asset can be defined as the present value of the stream of profits earned by that asset.
... their attempts to define a leisure business.

defined wird häufig in verkürzten Nebensätzen verwendet.
in the sense defined above
usually defined as ...

Eine Definition ist *a definition (of something). by definition* ist per Definition.

evidence. *evidence* ist das Material an Beobachtungen, Daten, das man für einen Beweis oder eine Begründung braucht. Das Wort wird nur im Singular und ohne den unbestimmten Artikel *an* verwendet.
Much empirical evidence contradicts this.
There is not a shred of evidence. ... kein Anzeichen von ...
the evidence is convincing
persuasive/little/weak/scant/strong evidence

evidence for ist Material für eine bestimmte Annahme. *evidence from* ist Material von einer bestimmten Quelle. *evidence of* (oder mit einem *that*-Satz) ist Beweismaterial, dass etwas so ist.

Material in Bezug auf ist *evidence on.*
evidence on trends in poverty
evidence on the Risk-Return Relationship

Verben mit *evidence* (Beweismaterial) als Objekt: *find* (finden), *discover* (entdecken), *present* (vorstellen), *provide, review* (kritisch zusammenfassen).
use as evidence etwas als Beweismaterial verwenden

Das Adjektiv *evident* und das Adverb *evidently* werden im Sinne von ‚offensichtlich, klar erkennbar' verwendet.

examine. *examine something* ist ‚untersuchen, überprüfen'. Hierzu das Substantiv *examination (of).*
examining a single firm in greater detail
The third service sector that McKinsey examined was the television.

find. *find* kann auch im Sinne von ‚durch Untersuchungen feststellen, ermitteln, dass' verwendet werden. In dieser Bedeutung verlangt *find* ein Objekt, das einen Untersuchungsgegenstand bezeichnet.
Im Unterschied dazu: *to find a job* einen Arbeitsplatz finden.
find als ‚untersuchen' kann mit einem *that*-Satz konstruiert werden, dieses *that* kann weggelassen werden (siehe zweites Beispiel).
McKinsey claims to have found evidence that ...
They found chief executives gained little from higher share prices Sie stellten fest, dass ...

finding. Mit *finding* wird ein ‚Ergebnis aufgrund von Untersuchungen' bezeichnet.
the adoption of those findings by the GATT council ... die Anwendung dieser Erkenntnisse durch ...
Some of the book's findings may come as a surprise ... dürften überraschend sein
the OECD's most striking finding is that ...

model. Innerhalb des wissenschaftlichen Sprachgebrauchs versteht man unter *model* (wie unter Modell) ein theoretisches Konstrukt, mithilfe dessen man Beobachtungen einordnet, erklärt und, wenn es gut geht, auch Vorhersagen machen kann.
the Berle-Means model
Keynes's simple preliminary model
Their model assumes that ...
standard economic models
standard exchange-rate models

Die Simulation kann als *computer model* bezeichnet werden.

Häufig wird *model* auch im Sinne von ‚Spielart, Erscheinungsform' verwendet, von einer detaillierten Theorie ist dann nicht die Rede.
the Japanese and German models of capitalism
the familiar west German model
the European model
the American model

Im Herstellungsbereich:
French car buyers, for example, can choose from around 700 models made by 60 manufacturers.

Das Verb *model (something on something)* ist ‚etwas auf der Grundlage von etwas gestalten'.
a European Central Bank modelled on the Bundesbank

professor. *professors* sind Professor(inn)en. Die entsprechende Universität wird mit *at* eingeführt, das Fach mit *of*.
professors and practical businessmen
a professor at London Business School
a professor of economics

Professor(inn)en an einer Universität: *professors at (Harvard University, Yale University)*. Werden die Betreffenden mit Namen genannt, steht *of: Stephen Ross of Yale University*.

proof. *proof* ‚Beweis' ist ein Singularwort, ohne den unbestimmten Artikel *a*. Es wird mit *of* oder einem *that*-Satz ergänzt. Siehe auch *evidence* in diesem Abschnitt.
No proof is needed.
the burden of proof die Beweislast
Is such pay moderation proof that supply-side reforms have made wages more responsive to labour-market conditions ... ?
Ms Tyson offers no such proof.

prove. Wenn man sagt: *someone/something proves* + *that*-Satz, dann wird etwas bewiesen.
Evidence of such trends does not quite prove that the market is inefficient, however.
In den Konstruktionen Substantiv + *prove (+ to be)* + Substantiv bzw. Adjektiv bedeutet *prove* ‚sich erweisen, herausstellen als'.
German unification has proved a mixed blessing for the rest of Europe.
His views on European integration have proved far-sighted.
But he has proved to be one of the Bank's toughest governors.

research Substantiv. *research* [rɪ'sɜ:tʃ] ‚Forschung, Forschungen' steht im Singular und ohne den unbestimmten Artikel *a*. Der Gegenstand der Forschung kann durch ein vorausgehendes Adjektiv oder Substantiv genannt werden.
chemical research
economic research
market research
Commodities Research Bureau
Auch *on* und *into* führen den Untersuchungsgegenstand ein.
The Institute for International Economics, a think-tank based in Washington, DC, recently commissioned research into 13 cases of radical economic change.
recent research on the effects of deregulation
Die Forscher selbst *(the researchers)* werden mit *by* eingeführt.
research by Edward Wolff

review. *a review* [rɪ'vju:] ist eine (kritische) Übersicht, ein informierender Überblick. Das Wort wird öfters in Titeln von Zeitschriften verwendet. Das dazugehörige Verb ist *to review* [rɪ'vju:].
Harvard Business Review
a review of studies by the OECD
Mr Krugman's review of the evidence is convincing.
It reviews several behavioural studies.

science/scientist/scientific. *science* (im Singular und ohne den unbestimmten Artikel *a)* ist ‚Wissenschaft (allgemein)'.
That is how science evolves. So entsteht Wissenschaft.

Mit *a science* bzw. *sciences* bezeichnet man eine bestimmte Disziplin oder bestimmte Disziplinen.
the physical sciences die naturwissenschaftlichen Disziplinen

science wird in der Regel im Sinne von ‚exakter Wissenschaft/Naturwissenschaft' gebraucht *(a precise science)* – Literaturwissenschaft, Kunstwissenschaft usw. sind keine *sciences*. Jedoch, Sozialwissenschaften sind *social sciences,* und man kann auch generell von *inexact sciences* sprechen.
Forecasting is an inexact science.

Da wirtschaftliche Abläufe oft von sehr vielen und schwer abwägbaren Faktoren beeinflusst sind, wird in Frage gestellt, ob man es, zumindest teilweise, mit „Wissenschaft" zu tun hat.
Can the study of management be 'scientific'?
the effort to construct a 'science' of management

a scientist ist ein Wissenschaftler, *scientific* ist ‚wissenschaftlich'.

study *verb*. Das in wirtschaftlichen Texten relativ seltene Verb *study something* kann ‚untersuchen' bedeuten.
In every sector they studied they predict a gain.

Das Partizip *studied* wird nur nachgestellt verwendet.
during the period studied während des untersuchten Zeitraums
in 12 of the 17 countries studied ... der untersuchten Länder

study Substantiv. Das Substantiv wird häufig verwendet: ‚Studie, Untersuchung'.

Die Verfasserschaft einer Untersuchung wird mit *by* zugeschrieben, auch, indem man Verfasser oder Veranlasser voranstellt.
a new study by Richard Beason
a recent study by Elliot Berg
the GATT study
the McKinsey study
the Friedman and Schwartz study

Was untersucht wird, wird mit *of* angeschlossen.
their studies of 'game theory'
a survey of studies of costs
in their classic study of money in America

Mit dem Anschluss *on* wird ein größeres Untersuchungsgebiet, meist ein allgemeineres Thema genannt. Wie das letzte Beispiel zeigt, ist allerdings der Unterschied zwischen *of/on* nicht zwingend.
a recent study on Latin America
studies on unemployment
a study on airport slot allocation

Adjektive, die mit *study* verbunden sind, sind z.B. *academic, classic, comparable, detailed, economic, empirical, new, previous* (‚früher'), *recent* (‚kürzlich erschienen'), *scientific, similar, systematic*.

Verben, die mit *study* als Subjekt auftreten, sind z.B.: *admit that* (‚zugeben'), *conclude that* (‚zu dem Ergebnis kommen'), *compare* (‚vergleichen'), *confirm that* (‚bestätigen, bekräftigen'), *contribute to* (‚beitragen'), *claim that* (‚behaupten, fordern'), *estimate that* (‚schätzen'), *find that* (‚kommen zu dem Ergebnis, dass'), *look at* (‚untersuchen'), *point out that* (‚weisen darauf hin, dass'), *prove that, reckon that* (‚rechnen damit, dass'), *show that, suggest that*.

survey Substantiv. *a survey* ['sɜːveɪ] ist ein Gutachten/eine Untersuchung, insbesondere dann, wenn das Material durch Befragung von Personen oder durch den Vergleich von Daten zustandekommt. Das Verb ist *to survey* [sə'veɪ].
public-opinion surveys
the Bank of Japan's survey of business confidence
a survey of studies of the costs ...
[They have] surveyed a wide range of recent research.

theory. Wie bei dem deutschen Wort ‚Theorie' gibt es einen wissenschaftlichen Gebrauch von *theory* und Verwendungen, die eher nicht fachsprachlich sind. Eine (wissenschaftliche) Theorie enthält bestimmte Grundannahmen, die dann ausgebaut werden und ihre Rechtfertigung dadurch erhalten, dass sie ein vorliegendes Verhalten erklären oder ein zukünftiges voraussagen können.
game theory die Spieltheorie
Keynes's most influential work, his 1936 'General Theory of Employment, Interest, and Money'
growth theory die Wachstumstheorie
Economic theory provides good reasons for deregulation ... die Wirtschaftstheorie

Das Wort wird teils als Singularwort (ohne den unbestimmten Artikel *a*) verwendet, teils aber auch mit *a* und als Plural *theories*. Im ersten Fall meint man damit eine allgemeine Theorie oder Theorie allgemein. Im zweiten Fall meint man eine Theorie in Bezug auf einen bestimmten, vergleichsweise engen Forschungsgegenstand.
'A Theory of Incentives in Procurement and Regulation'
these new growth theories
new theories about growth
Typically, these theories assume that ... Es ist typisch für diese Theorien, dass sie annehmen, davon ausgehen, dass ...

theory im wissenschaftlichen Sinn wird mit *about, of* oder einem *that*-Satz ergänzt. Die Art der Theorie kann auch durch vorgestellte Adjektive/Substantive bezeichnet werden.
options theory
game theory
public-finance theory
new theories about growth
the theory of contracts
The theory that under free trade, wages will tend to converge in different countries also has a ring of common sense about it.

Mit *of* werden auch diejenigen eingeführt, die die Theorien verfasst haben.
the new theories of John Law
the theories of economists

Verben mit *theory* als Objekt: *apply* (‚anwenden'), *adapt* (‚anpassen'), *confirm* (‚bestätigen'), *use* (‚verwenden'), *refute* (‚zurückweisen'), *publish* (‚veröffentlichen').

Verben mit *theory* als Subjekt: *claim* (‚behaupten'), *suggest* (‚vorschlagen'), *assume* (‚annehmen'), *require* (‚verlangen'), *rely on, be based on* (‚basieren auf'), *explain* (‚erklären').

Mit *in theory* wird bezeichnet, was „nur in der Theorie", nicht aber unbedingt in der Praxis funktioniert.
In theory, eastern Germany enjoys many advantages.
Einige der *theories* sind eher ‚Vorstellungen, Ideen'.
The theory that employers who believe workers are unlikely to stay will be more reluctant to train them.

ZAHLEN

Brüche. Höhere Brüche werden ausgeschrieben: *half a percentage point, a quarter of the figure.*

Dezimalzahlen. Dezimalzahlen werden mit einem Punkt (.) vor dem Zehntel geschrieben: *7.6%* (gesprochen: *seven point six percent*).

digit. a digit ['dɪdʒɪt] ist eine Ziffer. ‚Zweistellig' ist *double-digit.*
in the days of double-digit inflation in the 1970s and early 1980s ...
double-digit rates of unemployment

figure. Das Wort *figure(s)* bezieht sich auf Zahlen, Zahlenangaben:
the latest figures for the public-sector accounts
the true figure is over 12%
a quarter of the figure for 1997-98

Jahreszahlen. Jahreszahlen werden mit vier Ziffern geschrieben: *1997, 1989, 2000, 2010.*
Zweistellige Jahreszahlen treten nur in Verbindung mit vierstelligen auf: *in 1994-95.*

million, billion, trillion. Zahlen mit mehr als sechs Ziffern werden vermieden und mit Hilfe von *million* bzw. *billion* (=‚Milliarde'!) ausgedrückt. Das *million* wird

nicht ausgeschrieben, sondern als *m* unmittelbar an die letzte Ziffer gesetzt. Nach Zahlen werden *million* und *billion* im Singular gebraucht (nicht: *5 *billions*). Währungsangaben gehen voran. *a trillion* ist eine Billion (eine 1 mit 12 Ziffern 0).
$23.7 billion
5.3m tonnes
nearly $3 trillion
Gesprochen: *twenty-three point seven billion dollars; five point three million tonnes*

number. Das Wort *number* wird im Sinne von Anzahl, aber auch im Sinne von Zahl verwendet.
the number of unauthorised compact discs
Yet 1 billion people still have no clean water, 2 billion are without sanitation, and the same number have no electricity.
Other methods, based on the consumption of meat, poultry and other expensive foods, suggest much lower numbers.
It defines exports as the sum of three numbers ...

point. Ein (Prozent)Punkt ist *a (percentage) point*.
Sweden's central bank raised its overnight lending rate to banks by a savage six percentage points ...
Canadian banks lifted their prime lending rates by half a point, to 7.5%.
decimal point ist das Dezimalkomma.

Ungefähre Angaben. Zahlen können durch weitere Angaben „ungefähr" gehalten werden.
for about six years ... ungefähr ...
Sugar supplies are tightening worldwide and prices have climbed above 13 cents a pound. ... auf über ...
Copper rose above $2,700 a tonne. ... auf über ...
London Metal Exchange stocks have fallen below 2m tonnes. ... auf unter ...
15% below July's peak ... unter den Höchststand vom Juli
It has gained almost 10% ... fast ...
almost $154 billion
some 30,000 tonnes ungefähr ...
some 40% below
for nearly seven years fast, beinahe ...

nearly 40%
nearly $3 trillion
The department puts Brazil's 1995-96 crop at between 15.7m and 17.7m bags.
... zwischen ...
between 1976 and 1998

Veränderung in Zahlen. Siehe hierzu den „Hinweis: Verben und Ergänzungen" zu Beginn von STEIGEN, MEHR WERDEN ...

Vierstellig und aufwärts. Zahlen ab 10 000 werden durch ein Komma vor der dritten Zahl von hinten lesbarer gemacht. Das Komma wird nicht gesprochen.
200,000 tonnes 200 000
25,000 tonnes
Im allgemeinen wird das Komma auch bei Zahlen ab 1000 gesetzt: *$5,700 a tonne.*

ZEIT

Wirtschaftliche Vorgänge spielen sich, wie andere Vorgänge auch, in einer bestimmten Zeit ab. Es ist wichtig darstellen zu können, welche Entwicklungen zu welchem Zeitpunkt, über welche Dauer stattgefunden haben. Die sprachlichen Mittel, die dabei verwendet werden, entsprechen nicht immer denen, die man in der nicht-fachlichen Sprache einsetzt.
Die Formulierung zeitlicher Bezüge wird in den folgenden Abschnitten dargestellt.

1. Zeitspannen und Zeitpunkte

period (Zeitraum)
season (besonderer Zeitabschnitt)
year (Jahr)
Jahreszahlen
quarter (Quartal)
month (Monat)
Monatsnamen
week (Woche)
Tage

2. Zeitkonzepte

2.1 Gegenwart
2.2 Vergangenheit
2.3 Zukunft
2.4 Gleichzeitigkeit
2.5 Häufigkeit
2.6 Dauer

3. Präpositionen und Konjunktionen

after
at
before
by
during
in
on
since

4. Verbformen

simple past
present perfect

1. Zeitspannen und Zeitpunkte

period. *a period* ist ein Zeitraum. Das Wort wird fast immer mit weiteren Bestimmungen gebraucht. Die häufigste ist *in the same period* ‚im selben Zeitraum'.
Dies kann weiter eingeschränkt werden:
in the same period of 1998
in the same period in 1997
up by 77 % on the same period last year
Werden mehrere Zeiträume besprochen, kann man *in the second period* ‚im zweiten der erwähnten Zeiträume, Abschnitte', *in the first period* verwenden. *over the period, during the period* (‚während') setzen voraus, dass der Zeitraum aus dem Text bekannt ist.
Die Dauer des Abschnitts:
over the four-year period während ...
for a period of up to two years für den Zeitraum von bis zu zwei Jahren

Die Bestimmungen *in the same period* o.ä. stehen am Anfang oder am Ende des Satzes.

season. *season* ist, bei landwirtschaftlichen Produkten, die Ernte(zeit).
this season die diesjährige Ernte, in der diesjährigen Ernte
last season die letzte Ernte, in der letzten Ernte
next season die nächste Ernte, in der nächsten Ernte
the 1996-97 season die Ernte 1996-97

year. ‚Im gegenwärtigen Jahr' ist *this year.*
Nickel prices have doubled this year.
‚Diesjährig' ist *this year's.*
This year's best performer was Milan.

next year im kommenden Jahr
a year ago im vorigen Jahr
last year im letzten Jahr

Sei derzeit *(this year)* 1999, dann ist 1998 *a year ago* oder *last year* oder *a year earlier.*

Die häufigste Zeitbestimmung ist ‚bis Monat, Quartal des laufenden Jahres'.
in the year to October
in the year to August
in the year to the second quarter
China's GDP grew by 10.4% in the year to the third quarter.
Consumer-price inflation edged up in the year to October.

Unter Verwendung von *year* werden die folgenden Zeiträume bezeichnet:
for 40 years seit 40 Jahren
for nearly seven years
in the past few years
in the last four years
in recent years in den wenigen Jahren davor
over the past year (nicht: **over /during/ in the last year!*)
over the year
every year (since 19..) in jedem Jahr seit 19..
in the years from 1993 to 1995

Die Dauer wird auch durch Fügungen wie in *a four-year high* ausgedrückt.
Dem ‚jährlich' entspricht *annual*: *America's annual growth rate; Canada's annual GDP growth; Hungary's annual consumer-price inflation rate.*
‚Pro Jahr' ist *a year*: *a paltry 0.3% a year.*
Siehe auch anschließend „Jahreszahlen" und *month* (dort *12 months*) in diesem Teilabschnitt.

Jahreszahlen. Das jeweilige Jahr (nach der Zeitrechnung) wird über die vierstelligen Ziffern bezeichnet, also 1997, 1998, 2001. Die Angabe ‚im Jahr ...' ist immer *in* ..., also *in 1997, in 1998* (und nicht lediglich *1997, wie das im Deutschen möglich ist).
Die wichtigsten Verwendungen sind (eine genannte Jahreszahl steht dabei für andere):
in 1997, in 2005
in January 1986
by 1991, by (the year) 2000
after 1996
since 1990
since the start of 1996
at the beginning of 1985
at the end of 1995
since spring 1987
to end-1993
at the end of 1994
at the beginning of 1995
in early 1997
in late 1987
in mid 1994
in the first half of 1987
in the first quarter of 1996
until 1987
in the four years to 1996
in 1993-94
between 1986 and 1996

Dekadenbezeichnungen sind z.B. *the 1970s, the 1990s.*

Jahreszahlen können als Subjekt verwendet werden.
Yet 1990 was an exception.

quarter. *a quarter* ist ‚ein Vierteljahr, Quartal'. Die häufigsten Ausdrücke sind:
in the first (second, third, fourth) quarter
to the second, third etc quarter
in the year to the second (third, fourth) quarter
each quarter

Das Adjektiv ist *quarterly: a quarterly summary.*
(*a quarter* ist auch die Bruchzahl 1/4: *a quarter of the figure, three-quarters of a percentage point.*)

month. *a month* [mʌnθ] ist ein Monat, *12 months* sind ein Jahr (jedoch nicht im Sinne des Kalenderjahres). *this month* ist ‚in diesem Monat, diesen Monat'. Da Berichtszeiträume meist mehr als einen Monat umfassen, finden sich häufig Formulierungen mit Zahl plus *month.*
in the 12 months to August
in the same 12 months
in the first nine months
in the next three months
for six months
over the past few months

‚im selben Monat' ist *(in) the same month,* ‚im vorhergehenden Monat' ist *in the previous month.*
12-month wird als Adjektiv gebraucht.
a 12-month rise
a 12-month deficit
a 12-month growth rate

Monatsnamen. ‚im Oktober' ist *in October.* Die Monatsnamen sind erweiterbar durch eine Jahreszahl: *in December 1994.* Mitteilungen, die für einen bestimmten Monat gelten, sind *for.*
new reserve figures for November

Weitere Phrasen:
last September
next June

in late June
by the end of September
since September
in the year to September
in the 12 months to September

week. *a week* ist eine Woche, dieser Zeitraum spielt vor allem in Börsenberichten eine Rolle.
this week
last week
during the week
over the week
39% down on a week earlier im Vergleich zur Vorwoche

Das Adjektiv ist *weekly*. Fügungen wie *six weeks* können (mit Apostroph) adjektivisch gebraucht werden: *a six-weeks' rise*.

Tage. Einzelne Tage werden mit dem Monatsnamen und der Ordnungszahl bezeichnet. Die Präposition ‚am' ist *on*: *on October 1st, on September 22nd, on July 7th (,1998)*

2. Zeitkonzepte

2.1 Gegenwart

this. Die Fügungen *this week, this month, this season, this year* werden für ‚in dieser (jetzigen) Woche, in diesem (jetzigen) Monat usw.' verwendet. Man sagt nicht **in this week*. Mit Monatsnamen und Jahreszahlen steht jedoch *in*:
The seers are happier this month than in October.

Beachte die dazugehörigen Genitivformen: *Tel Aviv was this week's star performer.*

current. Die Bedeutung ‚derzeitig' kann durch *current* formuliert werden.
the current crop die derzeitige Ernte
current prices
the current rate

now. *now* ist ‚jetzt, derzeit'. Ist das verwendete Verb eine Form von *be,* steht das *now* nach dieser Form.
Britain has dropped to the bottom of the table. Its industrial output is now no higher than it was at the beginning of 1988.
Werden Hilfsverben verwendet, steht *now* nach dem ersten Hilfsverb.
The worry is that producers may now be tempted to start up idle capacity ...
Bei den übrigen Verben steht *now* vor dem Verb.
The number of businessmen who believe sales will rise in the fourth quarter of 1994 now exceeds the number who believe they will fall in all of the 15 countries in our chart.
Endstellung ist bei Betonung möglich:
The price of uranium has fallen from $10.50 a lb a year ago to $7 now.

present. Das Adjektiv *present* ist ‚gegenwärtig'. Der derzeitige Wert von etwas ist *the present value of something. at present* ist ‚derzeit, zum gegenwärtigen Zeitpunkt'.
the present approach
America's present rates of inflation and economic growth
That gives the present value of future profits.
No country at present satisfies the treaty's preconditions for EMU.

2.2 Vergangenheit

ago. Die häufigste Zeitangabe für eine vergangene Zeit ist *a year ago* ‚letztes Jahr, im vergangenen/letzten Jahr, im Vorjahr'. Die Fügung mit *ago* steht häufig direkt nach Zahlen oder nach Vergleichen.
America's retail sales fell in November, for the fourth consecutive month, and were 1.7% lower than a year ago.
The price of uranium has fallen from $10.50 a lb a year ago to $7 now.
Weiterhin: *three years ago, years ago.*

earlier. Wie bei *ago* ist die häufigste Verbindung die mit *year: a year earlier* ‚im Vorjahr'. Ein Unterschied zu *a year ago* besteht nicht. Weiterhin:
a week earlier
earlier this year

183

last. *last* plus *week, month, September, year* usw. ist ‚letzte Woche, letzten Monat usw.' (Nicht: **in the last week*).
Die Fügung *in the last four years* bezeichnet einen Zeitraum, ‚in den letzten vier Jahren'. Ohne Verwendung von Zahlen wird *in the last few years* gesagt. Man sagt nicht **in the last years,* siehe den anschließenden Eintrag *past.*

past. *past* ist als Adjektiv ‚letzt-, vergangen-', wie in
over the past 12 months
over the past decade
over the past week
over the past year
over the past five years
in the past few years
during the past four years

Die Präpositionen *in, during, over* weisen darauf hin, dass mit *past* Zeiträume bezeichnet werden (‚während'), nicht Zeitpunkte. Man kann nicht sagen *The contract was signed in the past year.*
Steht das folgende Substantiv im Plural *(years, months),* muss das *past* erweitert werden, z.B. mit *few, four, six: over the past five years.*
Siehe auch den vorhergehenden Eintrag *last.*

previous. ‚im Vormonat' ist *in the previous month.*
Weiterhin:
the previous month's figures
the previous month's forecast

since. Siehe „3. Präpositionen und Konjunktionen", dort den Eintrag *since.*

then. *then* als ‚damals' wird häufig mit *now* kontrastiert.
The Japanese inflation rate, then 2.6%, is now 3.6%.

‚Seit damals, seit dann, von da ab' ist *since then.*
Since then the rate of growth has declined.

2.3 Zukunft

Siehe auch die Abschnitte ERWARTEN, SCHÄTZEN, VORAUSSAGEN; PLANEN, BEABSICHTIGEN; *CAN – COULD – BE ABLE TO; MAY – MIGHT; WILL – WOULD; SHOULD.*

come. Am Anfang eines Satzes kann *Come October, ...* stehen oder *Come July (etc), ...* in der Bedeutung ‚kommenden Oktober usw.'

coming. *the coming months, years* sind die kommenden Monate, Jahre.
The peseta is unlikely to weaken much over the coming months.

due. Der Ausdruck in *due course* ist ‚wenn der Zeitpunkt dafür gekommen ist'.
due zusammen mit einer Zeitbestimmung oder einem Infinitiv mit *to* bedeutet, dass etwas (vereinbarungsgemäß) geschehen soll.
... with an election due next month ... bei Wahlen, die nächsten Monat bevorstehen
Germany's last remaining zinc mine is due to close in March. ... wird im März geschlossen.
Zu *due* in der Bedeutung ‚zurückführbar auf, begründet in' siehe *due to* in URSACHEN, FOLGEN, BEGRÜNDUNGEN.

next. *next year* ist ‚nächstes Jahr, im nächsten Jahr'.
Beachte: Man kann nicht sagen **the next months*.
Steht das Substantiv im Plural, muss *next* durch *few* oder ein Zahlwort erweitert werden: *over the next six months*.

future. *in the near future* ist ‚in der nahen Zukunft'.
Auch als Adjektiv, z.B. in: *future plans*.

2.4 Gleichzeitigkeit

meanwhile. *meanwhile* ist ‚inzwischen, in der Zwischenzeit, währenddessen'.
Es wird häufig als eine Art Zusatz (abgetrennt durch Kommas) verwendet.
Meanwhile, the D-mark's share rose to 19.7%; the yen's climbed to 8.7%.
Rapid growth in many Asian economies, meanwhile, helped to boost coal output by 11.8%.

Hinweis: Die Konjunktion *while* wird fast stets im Sinne von ‚während dagegen'
verwendet. Siehe hierzu *while* in GEGENSATZ, EINRÄUMUNG.

same. Zum Ausdruck der Gleichzeitigkeit wird *same* verwendet. Die Kombination
mit *period* ist bei weitem die häufigste.
in the same period
over the same period
in the same 12 months
in the same month
‚im selben Monat, im gleichen Monat' ist auch *the same month*.

still. Das Adverb *still* ist ‚(immer) noch'. Zu *still* am Anfang des Satzes siehe *still* in
GEGENSATZ, EINRÄUMUNG.
The four big European countries are still lagging.   ... liegen immer noch zurück.
*Western mine supply has already fallen by 35% from its peak in 1980, but is still too
high.*   ... ist aber immer noch zu hoch.
In the same month Swiss unemployment rose to the still modest rate of 0.7% ... auf
noch geringe 0,7%.

when. *when* (als Adverb und als Konjunktion) drückt eine Zeitangabe aus, keine
Bedingung. Man könnte es etwas umständlich umschreiben als ‚zum Zeitpunkt
von'. Dieses ‚zum Zeitpunkt von' führt zu verschiedenen Übersetzungen ins
Deutsche.
When should that rule be broken? Wann ... ?
Managers have some choice when to invest.   ... wann/zu welchem Zeitpunkt ...
That is when reformers will face the threat. Das ist der Augenblick, wo/da ...

Wenn im Hauptsatz und im Nebensatz das *present tense* steht, kann mit ‚wenn'
übersetzt werden.
*But when monetary policy is tightened and short-term interest rates rise, the yield
curve inverts.*
*In recessions public spending tends to be pushed up as unemployment benefits
increase; the process is reversed when the economy picks up.*   ... der Prozess verkehrt sich, wenn sich die Wirtschaft wieder erholt.

Dieses ‚wenn' im Deutschen ist aber dann mehrdeutig: ‚falls' oder ‚sobald (als)'.
Aus diesem Grund ist das ‚sobald' vorzuziehen, denn *when* bedeutet eben nicht
‚falls'. Der letzte Beispielsatz ist daher ‚... der Prozess verkehrt sich, sobald sich die

Wirtschaft wieder erholt'. (Auch wenn in manchen Fällen ein ‚falls' naheliegt.) Für die Sätze im *present tense* könnte man auch sagen, dass mit *when* etwas genannt wird, das erwartet wird – während man mit *if* etwas formuliert, das man setzt oder annimmt.

when kann einen Zeitraum angeben, ‚während'. Beachte, dass *while* in Wirtschaftstexten eher ‚während dagegen' ist. Siehe *while* in GEGENSATZ, EINRÄUMUNG.
[This is not] feasible when capital flows are unfettered. [Das ist nicht] machbar, solange der Kapitalfluss unbehindert bleibt.

Stehen Hauptsatz und Nebensatz im *past tense*, dann ist das *when* ‚als'.
When Ian Byatt announced a new price limit on July 28th ...
In 1992, when sterling left the European exchange-rate mechanism, investors' inflationary expectations jumped from 4% to almost 5.5%.

Nebensätze mit *when* können verkürzt werden.
In that case, they would already have discounted these events when making their spending plans. ... als sie ...
Die Konjunktion bezieht sich auf einen bekannten oder genannten Zeitpunkt im Sinne von ‚als', der *when*-Satz steht nach dem Hauptsatz oder davor.

yet. Das Adverb *yet* bedeutet ‚bislang'. Es wird aber nur in negierten Sätzen verwendet. In Verbindung mit einer Absicht, einem Zwang u.ä. bedeutet es ‚noch'. (Am Satzanfang ist die Bedeutung ‚dennoch', siehe *yet* in GEGENSATZ, EINRÄUMUNG.)
Nobody has yet drawn the logical conclusion.
It hasn't happened yet.
machines and methods yet to be invented ... die erst noch erfunden werden müssen

2.5 Häufigkeit

Siehe *since* in diesem Abschnitt, dort in „3. Präpositionen und Konjunktionen".

2.6 Dauer

Siehe *past* in diesem Abschnitt, dort in „2.2 Vergangenheit" sowie *for* und *since* in diesem Abschnitt, dort in „3. Präpositionen und Konjunktionen".

within ist ‚innerhalb eines Zeitraumes, einer Frist'.
Rich countries must comply with the new rules within a year.
Roughly half of America's unemployed find work within a month.

3. Präpositionen und Konjunktionen

after. *after* ist ‚nach' in Angaben wie *after September 1994*, auch wie in *after a denial by the government*, auch für Zeiträume wie in *after two months*.

Als Konjunktion ist *after* ‚nachdem'.
After the Fed raised their interest rates ...

Wenn das Subjekt des Nebensatzes mit dem Subjekt des Hauptsatzes identisch ist, steht gewöhnlich *after* plus Verb plus *-ing*:
After rising sharply, the dollar ...
... after growing steadily in the 1970s, the dollar ...

at. *at* wird verwendet als ‚am', wie in
at the beginning of (the season, 1997, last year)
at the end of ...

Siehe auch den Abschnitt *AT*.

before. *before* im Sinne von ‚vor' steht mit Zeitangaben wie *1998* oder *the end of the year*, auch zusammen mit Ereignissen wie in *before the collapse of the Soviet Union*.

by. Mit *by* wird angegeben, dass etwas (spätestens) zum genannten Zeitpunkt oder vorher geschieht, also ‚(bis) zu'.
by the end of September
by July next year
by the end of the 1996-97 season

during. In Börsenberichten wird diese Präposition (‚während') in der Regel zusammen mit *week* verwendet. Andere Zeiträume gehen gewöhnlich mit *over*. In Börsenberichten stehen Ausdrücke mit *during* gewöhnlich am Ende des Satzes, nach numerischen Angaben.
The dollar fell by 0.8% during the week.

In anderen Wirtschaftstexten kann *during* mit allen möglichen Zeiträumen kombiniert werden.
during 1997

during the 1980s
during the course of the year
during a recession

for. *for* bedeutet ‚die genannte Zeit lang', *for 14 years* ist also ‚14 Jahre lang, seit 14 Jahren'.
for seven years
for almost four years
for about four years
The average American today lives for 76 years.
Zusammen mit *time* dient *for* für ‚zum xten Mal':
for the first time since 1973
for the first time in 11 months
for the third month in a row zum dritten Monat in Folge

In einem Satz wie *Hong Kong touched a new low for the year, with a 3.8% fall over the week* ist *for the year* ‚dieses Jahr betreffend'.

in. *in* ist ‚in dem bezeichneten Zeitraum, während des bezeichneten Zeitraums'.
in that decade
in the mid-1970s
in the same period
in the past
in the near future
in 1990
in 1988-89
in the year to October
in the year to the second quarter
in the four years to 1987
in the first half of 1997
in the third quarter
in September
in the same month
in the previous month
in the next three months
in 18 months
in the first nine months
for the first time in 11 months

Hinweis: Zu *this year, this month* ‚in diesem Jahr, Monat' u.ä. siehe *this* in diesem Abschnitt, dort in „2.1 Gegenwart".
Siehe auch *over* in diesem Teilabschnitt sowie *within* in diesem Abschnitt, dort in „2.6 Dauer".

on. Die Präposition *on* wird in der Alltagssprache zeitlich wie in *on Tuesday* ‚am Dienstag' verwendet, oder wie in *on the evening of January 1st* ‚am Abend des 1. Januar'.

on kann jedoch auch als ‚im Vergleich zu' verwendet werden.
Britain's retail sales fell 0.7% in December, but were 1.2% up on the year.
Industrial output fell by 0.6% in Japan and 0.7% in France in October. In both countries, though, output was up on the year – by 4.6% in Japan and 4.7% in France.

over. *over* mit Zeitangaben ist ‚während', vor allem in Börsenberichten.
over that period
over a short period
over the same period
over the past year
over the past seven years
over the next three months
over the week

Siehe hierzu auch *present perfect* in diesem Abschnitt, dort in „4. Verbformen".

since. *since* ist ‚von dem genannten Zeitpunkt an bis jetzt, seit'. *since* braucht als Ergänzung eine Zeitangabe, die punktuell aufzufassen ist, also etwa *since December 1996*. Zu *for* wie in *for four years* siehe *for* in diesem Teilabschnitt.
since spring 1996
since 1973
since 1979-81
since mid 1982
since the end of last year
since November
since April
since the end of last year
since September 22nd

Der Zeitpunkt kann auch durch Nennung eines Ereignisses formuliert werden:
Coffee prices plunged this week to their lowest level since frosts hit Brazil's coffee-growing region in late June.
Germany's foreign assets have also plummeted in the past few years; since unification, Germany has run large current-account deficits to support the redevelopment of the eastern Länder.

‚Seit damals, seit dann, von da ab' ist *since then*.
Since then the rate of growth has declined.

Siehe hierzu *present perfect* in diesem Abschnitt, dort in „4. Verbformen".

Zu *since* in der Bedeutung ‚da, weil' siehe *since* in URSACHEN, FOLGEN, BEGRÜNDUNGEN.

4. Verbformen

Von besonderer Bedeutung ist die Unterscheidung zwischen *simple past* (z.B. *did, went, arrived*) und *present perfect* (z.B. *has/have done, has/have gone, has/have arrived*).

simple past. *In the year to August, America's retail sales rose by 5.2%; Britain's increased by 3.7% in the 12 months to September. America's industrial production was unchanged in September, but still 6.6% higher than a year earlier. In the 12 months to August, France's industrial output grew by 5.2% and Italy's by 12.3%.* Dieser Abschnitt erschien in *The Economist* vom 22. Oktober 1994. Es wird über einen vergangenen Zeitraum gesprochen, einen Zeitraum, der definitiv zu Ende ist *(in the year to August)*. Die Verbform, die hierfür verwendet wird, ist das *simple past (rose, increased, was, grew)*. Das *simple past* findet sich bevorzugt dann, wenn Adverbiale der Zeit auftreten, die sich auf Vorgänge in der Vergangenheit beziehen, wie z.B.
last year
last month
over the past year
in 1989
in spring
at the end of 1990

Jedoch sind solche Adverbiale nicht notwendig, das *simple past* bedeutet für sich bereits „Vorgang abgeschlossen".

present perfect. Formen wie *has grown, have been, has changed* werden als *present perfect* bezeichnet. Das *present perfect* wird für Vorgänge verwendet, die in der Vergangenheit begonnen haben und bis derzeit, also einschließlich der Gegenwart, andauern. Im folgenden Satz ist also von einem Wachstum seit sieben Jahren die Rede.

Over the past seven years the output of Japan's industry has grown faster than that of any other of the seven largest OECD members.

Anders dagegen:
Britain's broad-money growth quickened to 14.4% in the 12 months to November; its narrow-money growth slowed to 3.1%. Over the same period, Germany's broad money supply grew by 5.5%.

Diese Sätze stehen in einer *Economist*-Ausgabe vom Dezember. Der genannte Zeitraum ist abgeschlossen *(in the 12 months to November)*, daher steht hier das *simple past*.

Das *present perfect* tritt daher mit Zeitbestimmungen auf, die von der Vergangenheit bis zur Gegenwart reichen, z.B.

since then
since 1997
for four years
over the year
over the last four years

Sollte sich eine Angabe wie *for four years* auf vier vergangene Jahre beziehen, steht das *present perfect* nicht: *In December America's 12-month rate of consumer-price inflation slowed to 2.9% and Britain's to 2.6%. Both rates were the lowest for about six years.* [aus der Sicht des folgenden Januars]

Aber:
Nickel prices have doubled this year, thanks to strong demand for stainless steel. [das Jahr ist noch nicht vorbei]

The Lusaka stock exchange opened earlier this year. [dieser Vorgang, des Öffnens der Börse in Lusaka, ist vergangen]

Ohne Zeitbestimmung könnte man natürlich sagen *The Lusaka stock exchange has opened* – das Offen-Sein dauert ja noch an.

INDEX BEHANDELTER WÖRTER

able 45
about 9
be about to do something 9
what about ...? 9
above 10f
academic 167
accept 18
admit 69
admittedly 69f
affair 18
after 137, 188
ago 183
agree 102f
aim (Substantiv) 103
aim (Verb) 103
alarm 62
alarming 62
albeit 70
all but 40
allow 100
although 70
annual 180
anything but 40
appear 50
appreciate 118
argue 18
argument 19
article 167
as 137f, 148
as...as 148f
as if/though 149
ask 167
asset(s) 159f
assume 50f
assumption 51
at 24f, 188

bar 38
base 138
basis 26
bear (Substantiv) 37
bearish(ness) 37
because 138
because of 138
before 188
belief 51
believe 51f
billion 175
blame 138f
bond(s) 163
borrow 84
borrower 85
borrowing 84f
bull 37
bullish(ness) 37
business 39f
but 40, 70f
buy 41
buyer 41
by 43, 188

can 43f, 99
capital 45ff
carbon (dioxide) 135
cause (Substantiv) 139
cause (Verb) 139
choice 104
choose 103f
claim (Substantiv) 168
claim (Verb) 168
climb 118

come 185
coming 185
comparable 149
comparative 149
compare 149f
comparison 150
concede 71
condition 26f
consequence 139f
continue 123
contrary 71
contrast 71f
convince 19
convinced 19
convincing 19
cost (Substantiv) 85f
cost (Verb) 85
could 44f, 101
credit 86f
creditor 87
creep up 118
current 182

damage (Substantiv) 62
damage (Verb) 63
danger 63
dangerous(ly) 63
debate 19
debatable 19
debt 87
debtor 87
decide 104f
decision 105
decline (Substantiv) 124
decline (Verb) 124

define 168
definition 168
deny 19f
dependence 140
depend 140
dependent 140
design 105f
designer 106
despite 72
develop 168
development 168
difference 151
different 151
difficult 63
difficulty 64
digit 175
discuss 20
discussion 20
distinction 72
drop (Substantiv) 124f
drop (Verb) 125
due 185
due to 140f
during 188

earlier 183
earn 76
earnings 76
economic 47f
economics 48
economist 49
economy 48f
edge down 125
edge up 118
emphasis 20
emphasise 20
employ 11f

193

employee 12
employment 12
employer 12
environment 135
environmental 135
environmentalist 135
equity, equities 161
estimate (Substantiv) 52
estimate (Verb) 52
even 72, 151
evidence 169
examine 169
example 151f
expand 118
expect 52f
expectation 53
expenditure 87f
expense 88
explain 141

fall (Substantiv) 125
fall (Verb) 126
fast 128
fear (Substantiv) 64
fear (Verb) 64
fearful 64
fee 76
figure 175
finance (Substantiv) 61
finance (Verb) 60f
financial 61f
financially 62
find 169
finding 170

fiscal 129
follow 141
for 141, 189
forecast (Substantiv) 54f
forecast (Verb) 54
forecaster 55
force (Verb) 27
fuel 135
fund(s) 163
further 152
future 185

gain (Substantiv) 77
gain (Verb) 77
given 27
go up 119
goal 106
greenhouse 136
ground (Substantiv) 141f
ground (Verb) 142
grow 119
growth 119f

harm (Substantiv) 65
harm (Verb) 65
have to 30f
hence 142
however 72f
hurt 65

if 28ff
imply 142
important 20
importance 20
in 189
income 77f

increase (Substantiv) 120f
increase (Verb) 120
increasingly 120
indebted(ness) 87
inflation 82f
inflationary 83
in order to 106
intention 106
insist 20
insistence 20
in spite of 73
intend 106f
intent 106
interest (Substantiv) 83f
interest (Verb) 83
invest 88
investment 88f
investor 89
issue (Substantiv) 21
issue (Verb) 21

job 12f
jobless 13
jump 121

labour 12
last 184
lead 142
leap (Substantiv) 121
leap (Verb) 121
lend 89
lender 89
less 152
liability 90
like (Verb) 107

like (Präposition) 153
likely 55f
little 92f
loan 90
lose 94
loss 94f

many 96f
market 36
matter (Substantiv) 21
matter (Verb) 21
may 98ff
mean 142f
meanwhile 185
meet 30
mention 21
might 100f
million 175
model 170
monetary 101
money 101
month 181
more 153f
mortgage (Substantiv) 90
mortgage Verb) 90
mortgagee 90
mortgagor 90
much 97f
must 30f

narrow 127
necessarily 31
necessary 31
need (Verb) 31f
need (Substantiv) 32
negative 65

nevertheless 73
next 185
nonetheless 73f
now 183
number 176

on 37, 190
once 33
opinion 55
opposite 74
ought 116
outlook 56
over 10f, 190
owe 90f
owing to 143

past 184
pay (Substantiv) 78
pay (Verb) 91
payment 78f
period 178f
permit 100
persist 123
persistent(ly) 123
persuade 21
pick up 121
plan (Substantiv) 108
plan (Verb) 107f
plummet 127
plunge (Substantiv) 127
plunge (Verb) 127
point (Substantiv) 22, 176
point (Verb) 22
pointless 22
pollute 136
pollution 136

possibility 56f
possible 56
possibly 56
predict 57
prediction 57
present (Adjektiv) 183
previous 184
price 91f
probability 57
probably 57
problem 22, 65f
professor 170f
profit 79
profitability 79
profitable 79
proof 171
proposal 108
propose 108
proposition 108
prove 171
provided 32f
purchase 41
purchaser 41
purpose 108

quarter 181
question (Substantiv) 23
question (Verb) 23
quicken 128

raise 92, 121
rally 121f

reason 143f
reckon 57
recover 122
reflect 144
reflecting 142

remain 124
require 33
reqirement 33f
research 171
result (Substantiv) 144f
result (Verb) 144
return (Substantiv) 79f
revenue 80, 129
review 172
rise (Substantiv) 122
rise (Verb) 122
risk (Substantiv) 66f
risk (Verb) 66
riskiness 67
risky 67

salary 80
sale 41f
same 154, 186
scheme 109
science 172
scientific 172
scientist 172
season 179
security, securities 160
seem 58, 155
seer 58
self-employed 14
self-employment 13
sell 42
seller 42
share(s) 162
should 115f
shrink 127

similar 155f
similarity 156
similarly 156
since 145, 190f
slow (Verb) 128f
slow(ly) 129
sluggish 37
slump (Substantiv) 128
slump (Verb) 127
small 93f
so 145, 156
soar 123
speedy 128
stay 124
still 74, 156, 186
stock(s) 161f
study (Substantiv) 173
study (Verb) 172
such 157
suggest 23
suppose 58f
supposedly 59
survey (Substantiv) 173
survey (Verb) 173

talk (Substantiv) 23f
talk (Verb) 23
tax (Substantiv) 130f
tax (Verb) 129f
taxable 131
taxation 131
taxman 131
taxpayer 131
tend 59
than 157

195

thanks to 145	unemployed 14	when 34, 186f	worry (Substantiv) 69
then 184	unemployment 14f	whereas 75	
theory 174f	unless 34	while 75	worry (Verb) 68f
therefore 145f	unwilling 111	why 146	worrying 69
this 182	unwillingness 111	widen 123	worth (Adjektiv) 147
though 74		will 163f	
threat 67	value (Substantiv) 146	willing 111	worth (Substantiv) 147
threaten 67f		willingness 111	
to (+ Inf.) 109	value (Verb) 147	within 187	would 165f
too 158	view 60	work (Verb) 15	
trend 59f		work (Substantiv) 15f	year 179f
trillion 175	wage(s) 80f		yet 75, 187
trouble 68	want 110	worker 16f	yield (Substantiv) 81
try 110	warn 68	workforce 17	
	warning 68	working (Substantiv) 17	yield (Verb) 81f
underemployment 14	way 158		
	week 182		